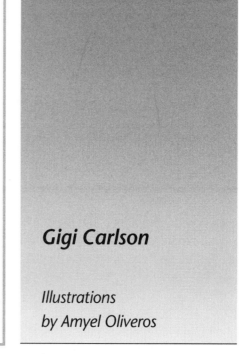

Gigi Carlson

Illustrations
by Amyel Oliveros

Digital Media in the Classroom

Increase the Learning Potential of Today's Digital Generation

CMP**Books**

San Francisco

For Celso and Tonino

Published by CMP Books
an imprint of CMP Media LLC
600 Harrison Street, San Francisco, CA 94107 USA
Tel: 415-947-6615; FAX: 415-947-6015
www.cmpbooks.com, email: books@cmp.com

Managing editor: Gail Saari
Copyeditor: Hastings Hart
Interior design and composition: Leigh McLellan
Cover design: Damien Castaneda

Distributed to the book trade in the U.S. by:	Distributed in Canada through:
Publishers Group	Jaguar Book Group
1700 Fourth Street	100 Armstrong Avenue
Berkeley, CA 94710	Georgetown, Ontario M6K 3E7 Canada
1-800-788-3123	905-877-4483

For individual orders and for information on special discounts for quantity orders, please contact:

CMP Books Distribution Center, 6600 Silacci Way, Gilroy, CA 95020
Tel: 1-800-500-6875 or 408-848-3854; Fax: 408-848-5784
Email: cmp@rushorder.com; Web: www.cmpbooks.com

Library of Congress Cataloging-in-Publication Data

Carlson, Gigi.
   Digital media in the classroom : increase the learning potential of today's digital generation / Gigi Carlson.
      p. cm. — (Digital media academy)
   Includes index.
   ISBN 1-57820-241-8 (alk. paper)
1. Computer animation. 2. Three-dimensional display systems. 3. Cinema 4D XL. 4. Computer graphics. I. Title. II. Series.
   TR897.7.P69 2004
   776'.6—dc22   2004012754

Printed in the United States of America
04 05 06 07   5 4 3 2 1
ISBN: 1-57820-241-8

Digital
Media
Academy

NEW HARTFORD PUBLIC LIBRARY

The Digital Media Academy is a premier technology training company offering a variety of courses in topics including web design, video production, 3D, digital media for the classroom, motion graphics, and game design. Courses are open to educators, teens, and adult learners. DMA instructors include nationally recognized technology experts and award-winning teachers. All DMA courses are offered for optional Stanford University Continuing Studies credit.

DMA is best known for its summer programs at prestigious locations like Stanford University. Each summer, hundreds of teens and adults attend one or more five-day immersion courses. DMA summer programs feature optional on-campus housing and dining and state-of-the-art facilities, all in a relaxed, collaborative environment.

DMA also provides on-site training to educational institutions and companies through its DMA on the Road program. Courses are customizable and available in any length from one to five days or more.

For more information about DMA and to register, call (toll-free) 866-656-3342, email info@digitalmediaacademy.org, or visit our website at www.digitalmediaacademy.org.

Contents

Acknowledgments

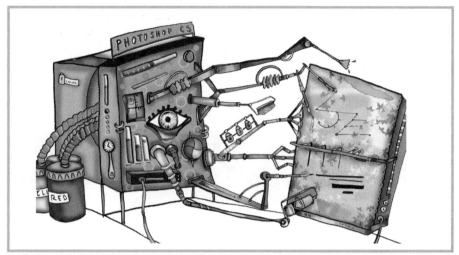

Many friends and colleagues were very supportive in the development of this book. I am grateful to Phil Gibson for elevating a course at the Digital Media Academy into a stand-alone book. Paul Temme and Dorothy Cox for finding ways to make publishing a fulfilling experience. Susan McLester, my editor, for building on the vision of innovative learning with technology. Anabel Jenkins, Ph.D., for writing the introduction. Cynthia Mauricio and Judith Crowther, Ph.D., for reading the drafts and giving me constructive feedback. Peggy Kleikamp and Taun Relihan, Ph.D., for teaching me about education in America. Aireen de Peralta, Beth Corwin, Sandy Novak, Lisa Deakes, and Anne Powers for keeping me abreast with technology, and Karen Strickholm on the business of writing and communications. Dessa Quesada for collaborating in a common vision of empowering teens with creative pedagogy and technology. Dean Constantine for providing invaluable legal guidance. Aurora Nagtalon and Denise Brown for warmth and support. Sari Carunungan for prayers. Tony Carlson, for the photographs used in the book. Victor Oliveros, for being my best technology teacher. Amyel Oliveros, for working late nights and weekends to complete the illustrations of the book. Finally, to my middle and high school students and fellow teachers who keep me learning and growing.

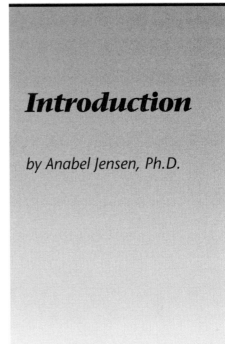

Introduction

by Anabel Jensen, Ph.D.

In teaching it is the method and not the content that is the message …
the drawing out, not the pumping in.　　—Ashley Montague

Seven Reasons for Buying and Using This Book

While I would not consider myself a technophile in any sense of the word, as an educator, a psychologist, a presenter and trainer, I believe I recognize outstanding and excellent pedagogy. This book is exactly that—providing both content and process.

Reason 1: The book unleashes the power of creative technology as a potent educational tool in a very practical and meaningful way within a classroom setting. The exercises bring to the fore the transforming and engaging capability of technology, so that students learn enjoyably and meaningfully.

When I performed Gigi's exercises, where she provides teachers with steps on how to familiarize students with various web search strategies, such as finding information on "purple frogs" or images of "inverted Ys," I realized the web provides me with data that would not be possible to find in an encyclopedia. For example, I can find my own name online and discover something about myself that is accessible to the inquiring world. Students will be intrigued by the accessibility of volumes of such information.

Reason 2: When I discuss with beginning teachers or pre-service teachers the importance of using technology in the classroom, many respond with, "Why do I have to teach technology when students know more than I do?" This book reduces hesitant teachers' fears of technology by providing keys (i.e., dynamic techniques and effective strategies) that will open the treasure troves of digital information. The book contains unique and unusual, as well as very practical, strategies for teachers to complement their classroom teaching. The exercises are concrete and sequential, guiding teachers through every aspect of the activity along with the procedural steps necessary for accomplishing a task requiring both software and hardware. Teachers will find this book user friendly.

Reason 3: The user guidelines are further enhanced by the use of Gigi's Helical Learning strategy, a much-needed road map of progressive activities for achieving subject matter mastery. Specifically defined, it is a learning helix comprised of four learning milestones: play, explore, integrate, and imagine. What is significant about the Helical Learning strategy is its ability to take students from simple to complex learning stages by engaging them in a series of hands-on projects. Also, the strategy provides a bridge between prior knowledge and new data by generating provocative questions. These lead students to participate in reflective discussions that create, generate, and stimulate thoughtful theorizing. Students' critical and creative thinking will grow exponentially.

Reason 4: Unfortunately, many students are unable to respond productively and enthusiastically to complex class projects, causing high frustration among their teachers. A deeper analysis of the situation reveals that this often happens when teachers are unable to provide students with step-by-step expectations and a dynamic process that enables them to envision the completion of their projects. Furthermore, the learning context becomes even more complex because of the differing levels of ability among students in every classroom. Then, teachers often question the viability of hands-on, project-based learning approaches for achieving "higher academic knowledge."

Instead, Gigi familiarizes the teacher with the nature of professional software and hardware and connects these to the parallel nature within the brain of the process of mental organization. For example, in the moviemaking module, where students create storyboards out of clay, Gigi uses children's toys as educational tools to help students conceptualize and organize story development. After students create their storyboards with clay and shoot them from various angles with a digital video camera, students then capture and trap the storyboard images to the video editing software by using a non-linear interface. After this they are able to sort them sequentially in the appropriate timeline. The activities enable teachers to tap into the potentials of students by bridging previous experiences to new knowledge. Students' imaginations will soar because they have parameters to keep them grounded and the freedom to explore.

Reason 5: Teachers are provided with multiple opportunities to create "authentic assignments" instead of artificial lessons. The module on creating a movie documentary where students are instructed to interview their peers about the effects of fast foods on their health connects the study of food nutrients and chemicals with real life issues. Teachers challenge their students through positive peer pressures. As producers of the documentary, the students build intrinsic motivation for learning about nutrition, food, obesity, and chemical elements. Learners undergo the same learning process as professional documentary filmmakers. In the end, the experience and technology enable them to become experts of the subject matter. Students who reach conclusions through a real life situation will apply the learning more readily.

Reason 6: One of the greatest concerns of teachers is the inability of students to focus appropriately on class activities. The bombardment of interactive media has inevitably shortened attention spans. Without extrinsic motivation to stir their curiosity and focus, students are unlikely to become involved.

However, in her module on interactive games, Gigi brings the teacher into the context of the gaming world. By becoming players rather than supervisors, teachers are able to gain first-hand experience in the fastest growing competition to homework completion. Then, with this foundation, teachers capture the energy and process of the gaming world and transfer it to the cognitive world by asking students to create their own interactive games, but with an academic base.

As teachers observe their students both creating and playing these interactive learning games in the classroom, they will note there is passion involved in their students' responses. Previously insecure and fearful students are stimulated by the active learning environment and are able to set aside their anxieties and inhibitions and become involved. Students' intrinsic motivation will be stimulated by the use of their personal voices.

Reason 7: Designed as easy-to-follow lesson plans based on national education standards, the activities provide students with critical frameworks for increasing their knowledge base. The inquiring, clarifying, summarizing, and predicting tools will empower students to deal with the more complex questions, plus the requisite problem solving, of higher academics. Students will be well prepared for the next developmental step. Also, teachers will adhere to district, state, and national standards with creative state-of-the-art methods.

Are you interested in moving your classroom from the 20th to the 21st century? This is a book you must have. Your students will love and appreciate you for buying and using it.

Anabel L. Jensen, Ph.D., is Associate Professor at Notre Dame de Namur University and President of Six Seconds (www.6seconds.org), a non-profit organization offering resources on emotional intelligence. She has been Executive Director of The Nueva School, Hillsborough, California for 15 years.

In 1998 my two sons, Victor, then 12 years old, and Amyel, 10, won an international Internet competition called the Junior Summit sponsored by the Massachusetts Institute of Technology (MIT) Media Lab.

Since Victor and Amyel were minors, I was offered the privilege of accompanying them to the conference where I watched young techies from over 90 countries dabble with computers, Lego blocks, robotic toys, and every imaginable technological gizmo. I was stunned by the sense of ease and excitement they exuded in this digital environment. I realized that these young people represented a new and fast-emerging breed of humanity in the modern world, called the digital generation.

As a parent, I was concerned that my children were increasingly bored with their classes in school. Already, they were exhibiting signs of common teenage maladies even before they were in high school. I was also concerned about the possibility of negative peer pressure.

Realizing the power that technology exerted in the lives of these students and inspired by discussions with MIT professors and parents of the other children at the Junior Summit, I initiated an experimental after-school program. Drawing upon my experiential learning, multimedia, and theater arts backgrounds, I launched a course where creativity, project-based learning, and technology were combined in a fun, project-oriented, peer-to-peer cooperative learning environment.

The pilot began with 10 students aged 10 to 15 years. I facilitated three-hour, weekly, and hands-on workshops that encouraged dynamic discussions, technology instruction, and inventive projects on topics that matter to teenagers. In my interactions with my sons and their school friends, I realized how little schools are able to address the emotional quotient so important in the life of a teen. These concerns include love, sex, identity, empowerment, peer pressure, depression, the generation gap, anger, and, of course, anything considered cool and hip. I thus sought creative and enjoyable ways to build intrinsic motivation for learning and zest for discovery and invention among my teen participants. The pilot was an active way to define curricular strategies with teenagers, linking their emotions and intrinsic motivation to academic achievement.

After three months of working together, the young techies came up with two recommendations. First, they wanted to create a web site called Visual Chat. These teens were concerned that only those who were able to write English could participate in chat sites on the web (at that time). To respond to language limitations of chat sites, they wanted to create a set of visual symbols that expressed a variety of emotions and ideas. They wanted to design a unique web language just for teens and by teens. In this way, youth from all over the world who speak different languages would be able to connect with each other.

The students, to my surprise, loved writing exercises. Considering the complaints from many teachers about the difficulty of inspiring teenagers to write during class time, I was amazed at how these teens craved writing projects. As a result of their interest in writing as a way to express their ideas and emotions, they also wanted to build a story-building site. This web site would provide an interface where teens from all over the world could collectively write stories. The site was to be designed so that, for example, a teenager in Norway could begin writing the story with a line or paragraph, then a teenager in Brisbane would add on to the introduction. Another teenager, perhaps from the U.S., would add the next line or paragraph, and so on. When the story neared its conclusion, teenagers from all over the world might write their own ending, making the story global and multidimensional.

In the summer of 1999, the 10 teenagers enrolled in a standard Create Your Own Web Site program at a neighborhood computer academy. For three months, these students sat behind computer workstations and pretended to be listening to the teacher. While writing with his marker, the teacher would constantly speak to the whiteboard, believing that his high school students were actually paying attention to what he had to say. A cursory check of their notebooks revealed notes from the lesson in the form of doodles. Clearly, a teacher who simply wrote instructions about software tools did not stimulate these kids. This teacher was unable to stir interest and get the students engaged in exploring the facets of software. I observed for a number of sessions, and I could see that there was no real interaction between the learners and the teacher in this classroom. The students' response to this teacher-oriented learning environment was non-productive when compared to the excitement generated as they dabbled with software and engaged in fun, hands-on, creative exercises.

I told the students that with the kind of attitude they showed in their software classes, we might as well end the program. Sensing my disappointment, the teens came up with a proposal. They said if I agreed to provide them with creative exercises and facilitate the learning process, they were going to find ways to learn software on their own as a group. I couldn't refuse their offer. We had a deal.

At this juncture of the program, my husband, Tony, who was then creative director of our multimedia company, took on the role of creative adviser for the kids' projects. He exposed them to a variety of artistic styles in multiple software applications and output formats such as print, web, animation, and video. Tony constantly challenged the kids' aesthetic sensibilities, and as they worked on their designs, he also helped them make creative decisions.

Eventually, the kids began working entire weekends. They insisted that three hours a week was just not enough time for them to accomplish the goals they had set for themselves. Our family weekend time was spent in the studio. The surprise was that at the end of four months, these students produced eight web sites, each one representing a topic of interest for today's youth, formulated from their unique teen perspectives.

In the process of building these sites, these 10- to 15-year olds accomplished what they had promised they would: to learn software on their own, while they worked on their projects, developing expertise in Microsoft Word and PowerPoint, Adobe Photoshop, HTML, and some Java.

The success of this experience hinged largely on a learner-centered, creative, challenging, and enjoyable pedagogy, allowing students to engage in hands-on exploration and experimentation with digital media tools. While they complained a lot about the way manuals were written, the kids used print references and software learning web sites when in desperate need to come up with solutions for their desired applications. To a great extent, they were in control of their learning. Tony and I supported their individual and group goals by listening to their ideas and tribulations, while helping them find realistic and innovative solutions.

Computer software and hardware became fascinating tools with which to articulate their visions, discuss issues, and showcase their talents. Ultimately, the pilot and their web sites became a venue where they proved their technological abilities. It also served as the "cool" way to connect with their friends. These kids were so motivated that the year in which they participated in the pilot, they achieved the highest academic grades of their entire school careers.

The successes of the program spurred me to further test and develop this budding pedagogy. In the next six months, I worked with Tony and with an artist-teacher colleague, Dessa Quesada, and the 10 teens as co-facilitators. We conducted similar programs with 500 hundred high school and 50 middle school students who came from a mix of schools. While each of the students had their own unique responses to the activities, the experience revealed no striking differences in their reactions to technology. They just loved working and learning with computers.

With the world rapidly changing it is virtually impossible for our generation of teachers to wrestle with the latest digital media tools used by the K–12 generation. For most, K–12 teaching already tends to take over our evenings and weekends. There is almost no time for teachers to study new software that fascinates our students. Yet the nature of interactive media and the vast information highway opens unprecedented opportunities to evolve new ways of teaching.

As a parent, I consider school the primary gateway to successful future careers of our children. Hence, at the rate technology is changing the landscape of our day-to-day lives and economic practices, it is imperative for educational leaders to integrate effective ways of teaching cutting-edge learning in the classroom to prepare today's students for the professional demands of the 21st century.

Knowledge Worker

Knowledge worker is a term born out of the technology revolution where access to and analysis of information has become a decisive variable in positioning a company, organization, or product in the global marketplace. These individuals are today's movers in industry, education, social development, and politics. They access information and transform it into value-oriented products, concepts, strategies, and services. While the term *knowledge worker* primarily refers to code developers in technology companies, the same concept and responsibility is vested in people who comprise the think tanks of public and private organizations and institutions.

It was from this invaluable experience and the 21st century concept of knowledge workers that I developed the educational strategy called Helical Learning. While getting high grades was one of the positive results of the pilot, the more important concern I had as an educator was to prepare students to be successful professionals by nurturing their talents and bringing them to the level of knowledge workers.

With this strategy, the right kind of learning environment nurtures students' abilities to conduct systematic research, analyze information, solve problems, and create value-oriented solutions. Helical Learning involves students in learning from real issues and problems and stimulates students to learn as authors, producers, publishers, designers, and entrepreneurs. In the 21st century classroom, the role of the teacher shifts from content lecturer to facilitator of the learning process and content-based digital media producer as collaborator in the conceptualization and development of innovative projects. The teacher becomes a catalyst of proactive learning.

Meaningful Innovative Learning

There were two other concerns that defined the pedagogy I designed for the pilot program. First, the unequal academic and emotional levels of the students and second, the need to connect their learning with real-life matters.

My early theater training and experience in the ninth grade deeply influenced my sense of knowledge acquisition. As theater artists, we were trained to develop script ideas and internalize characters in plays from a sensory and personalized approach. It was through this experience that I realized how much more interested I was in a subject matter when I went through a simulated experience about a topic. For example, there is a stark difference between being asked to describe a sour taste as compared to biting into a lemon. Its intense, tangy, acidic taste permeates through one's whole being and thereafter, a teacher can expect her students to describe sour taste in more words than can fit on the whiteboard.

By creating simulated experiences such as biting into a lemon, I can now relate the concept of sour beyond the lemon itself. It could also be a feeling, a reaction, or a moment. Moreover, sour is no longer only a kind of taste, but a memory that pertains to the intense, tangy, acidic feeling one may have experienced with personal loss, desperation, or stress. What might be a simple definition of sour in a vocabulary exercise is now connected to the students' personal experiences.

With a collective simulated experience, the students were on an almost equal playing field. Those who were not abstract learners in the class could now actively participate in building or contesting the subject matter. Additionally, the first-hand experience allowed them to bring in fresh insights about the topic whether or not they excelled in math, science, or language arts.

The other key component of the learning strategy was asking students open-ended and challenging questions that prompted them to respond as thinkers and not just as followers. For example, "What if Einstein was mistaken about the theory of relativity…?" I encouraged students to consider theoretical precepts as changeable by virtue of the changes in the variables that brought about these conclusions. I called on students when they succumbed to silence and daydreams. I encouraged them to question everything, that is, as long as their questions pertained to some real basis of doubt. Through simulated experiences, everyone could think of themselves as Einstein or Da Vinci in class.

Knowledge And Change

One of the most valuable lessons I empowered these students with is that *change is inevitable*. I would tell them, "What you may have thought of as correct today can be different tomorrow. So for your own sake, learn to be open-minded and flexible."

In a lecture-oriented pedagogy, the premise is almost always that the teacher is correct and book knowledge is superior to students' intelligence. All they are expected to do is to listen, memorize, fill in the blanks, and pass tests. As teachers, we are familiar with classroom situations where mostly two or three students respond to our questions while the rest ride the wave of passing high school by cramming and memorizing for tests. Research shows that most students remember only 20 percent of what they studied right after testing, far less I imagine than through knowledge acquisition experiences that impact their lives.

Learning And Interactive Games

Helical Learning highlights the potential of interactive gaming as a dynamic educational exercise. Unfortunately, among the more popular inventions today are a host of phenomenally-designed and coded computer and video games, and most of these tend to be violent, sexually oriented, and void of useful content. Most computer games become distractions to accomplishing school assignments.

The concept of "opposing forces" and "winning" reflects real-life dynamics whether this is in simple or complex situations. The ability to predict results through calculated risk strategies prepares students to emotionally and mentally face up to daily struggles encountered by people, organizations, and nations.

The Nash Equilibrium, for which noted mathematician John Nash won his Nobel Prize, takes off from the framework of strategy games. Along with mathematicians Neumann and Morgenstern, they argued that "a new theory of games was the proper instrument with which one can develop a theory of human behavior" (Sylvia Nasar, *A Beautiful Mind* [Touchstone Books, 2001]). By developing the gaming theory, mathematicians and economists are able to calculate and reflect people's decision-making patterns and determine winning military strategies.

Students in the pilot program, in addition to the 550 who participated in the workshops, were all very shy and quiet at the commencement of the course. They were silenced by their anxieties in a new environment with new faces. Immediately, this emotional lock was released by the socially oriented, face-to-face games that progressively drew them out of their zone of discomfort and acknowledged them as members of a positively competitive peer community.

What matters most is that with an interactive classroom, students are challenged and excited to become subject matter experts. Moreover, their appreciation of knowledge is further enhanced by their own abilities to review, contest, and enhance concepts and theories from their own collective and hands-on experiences.

Research-Based Learning

Another key component of the program was research; however, data gathering and analyses were done in very non-traditional ways. I wanted the kids to value information gathering, analyses, and writing without the stigma of what students call boring research activities. By participating in fun and competitive research-oriented games, students searched the web like it was a gadget of information. In every step of the way, they were intrigued by what they discovered. The activities were designed to excite them about seeking the best and most relevant information that could influence the results of their projects.

Students Learn More as Peer Teachers

The second part of the program involved the 10 pilot students as peer teachers. For this phase, I encapsulated the one-year out-of-school program into a two-day weekend course. There were two courses: Design Entrepreneur and Facilitators' Training. These 10 students took the second course in preparation for their role as peer facilitators. Tony, Dessa, and I taught them how to speak in front of an audience, create rapport with their peer participants, promote cooperative learning, and team up participants in groups so they are given the opportunity to meet as many co-participants as possible. We also showed them how to encourage participation, analytical thinking, and proactive learning; and create a happy and fun learning environment. At this point, these teens already knew the software (better than we did at times). We assigned two teen peer teachers for each of the classes and we acted as program supervisors.

After facilitating their initial workshops, the 10 teen trainers reflected that they had a better appreciation of the role teachers play in class. Our dialogues with the teaching teams during breaks were initially about their frustrations with peer participants. We reminded them that as facilitators, they needed to perform as professionals and that if they wanted to become successful professionals, they had to embrace their responsibilities, overcome irritants, and not be cowed by disappointments.

We saw how much effort the teen facilitators exerted to overcome their own fears of peer pressure. More important, they recognized how much they matured as teenagers. They saw how the negative traits of teens prohibited them from achieving the goals of an activity. They also realized how easy it is for teens to learn software and, at the end of the two days, how much fun it was to be able to peer teach and share skills with fellow youth.

While the experience did not completely resolve emotional issues faced by these teens, it opened their minds to the bigger world of professionalism and strengthened their beliefs in their abilities. They learned what professional responsibilities meant in reality, rather than in theory, as it would have been in lecture-oriented and teacher-centered classrooms. They had to deal with their individual emotional upheavals, which, by virtue of being teenagers, at times tended to get in the way of their responsibilities.

The Web and the Students' Web Site

At the end of the pilot program, the participants, then aged 11 to 17 years old, were launched as young professional web designers and writers with the support of Intel and Hewlett Packard. While financial limitations prevented us from maintaining a by-teens-for-teens web site, the experience enthused the young learners about the challenging and fast-changing world of media and communications. To date, the students are pursuing college degrees in fields where their tech-savvy experiences have made a difference in their performances.

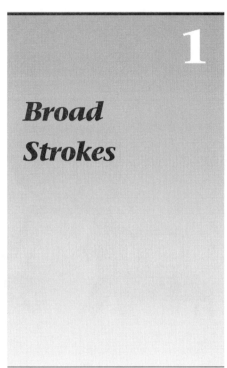

1

Broad Strokes

■ *Imagine …*
A 15-year-old student is leading a creative group of writers, designers, and publishers producing a short-story series to be distributed on the web.

■ *Imagine …*
A group of girls in high school and elementary school are working with an adult CEO of a gaming company in a boardroom. The students are presenting a new concept for an online game designed for girls aged 6–9 years old in a gaming market monopolized by boys.

■ *Imagine …*
Teams of middle school students are presenting a movie called *What It Takes to Survive Middle School* as an entry to a community festival of young moviemakers.

■ *Imagine …*
Students in fourth and fifth grades are taking pictures of tableaus made of clay with a digital camera and using Adobe Photoshop and Microsoft PowerPoint to share stories about themselves and their families in multimedia presentations.

■ *Imagine …*
Students are enthusiastically working on their class projects. Guided by their teacher, they are able to integrate insights with academic content, which follows national education standards. They work with their teams for weeks and learn about history, math, language arts, science, art, sports, and music, using state-of-the-art digital media tools. They build on each other's ideas and work like professional teams. As they master the subject matter, they form unique ideas to create changes and help their communities.

■ *Imagine …*
How much learning takes place when students are challenged to create value from knowledge. Learning is driven by hands-on experience and technology, which accelerates the processing and accessing of knowledge. The pedagogy highlights the abilities of young, tech-savvy, imaginative, and entrepreneurial learners.

■ ***Imagine … this … could be your classroom.***

Making the Book and DVD Work for You

Digital Media for the Classroom stimulates critical and creative thinking in young learners, through the educational strategy called Helical Learning. This is an innovative approach that motivates students in real world learning activities using technology.

Helical Learning engages students to learn as authors, designers, publishers, inventors, and entrepreneurs while exploring the possibilities they can generate with new digital media tools. Each of the activities presented is designed to optimize educational experiences with the interactive, content-rich and open-ended nature of digital media.

Digital Media for the Classroom enables teachers to develop their capabilities in the use of a variety of software, such as the Internet, interactive games, desktop publishing, Web design, and digital accessories including still and video cameras, microphones, lighting systems, scanners, and printers, to increase the learning potential of today's digital generation. The activities integrate professionally-oriented software with academic lessons, based on content standards in math, physical and social sciences, language arts, and the visual arts.

Additionally, to prepare students to succeed in the information age, proactive and project-based activities develop their skills in problem solving, collaboration, and effective communication.

Digital Media for the Classroom also provides teachers with guidelines to develop dynamic classroom curricula integrated with state-of-the-art digital media.

The Book

K–12 teachers interested in transforming their classrooms into 21st century learning centers will find cutting-edge, standards-based, and easy-to-use digital media projects and activities in this book.

Part 1 imparts the vision and methodology of Helical Learning and the context it evolved in.

Part 2 provides a host of hands-on multimedia projects and activities. Each of the projects includes pedagogy, content, organization, and technology—the four fundamentals of an effective 21st century curriculum. There are guides provided for applying these projects to specific grade levels and content areas.

The CD-ROM

The accompanying CD-ROM provides users with a multimedia gallery of sample projects based on the exercises in the book. These projects demonstrate the creative integration of a variety of software and hardware for use with with academic content.

Helical Learning in the 21st Century Classroom

Helical Learning is a strategy in which the classroom becomes like a professional working environment. Students study academic concepts and find solutions to serve their communities by creating alternative and improved products and services. Academic learning is likened to real world challenges. By participating in hands-on activities and using cutting-edge media, students develop a better sense of themselves as individuals capable of providing proactive and viable contributions to the world. The affirmation of their capabilities in this regard prepares students to succeed in future professions.

To further expound on this strategy, the following are sample scenarios of this competency-building environment.

The learning environment simulates professional work environments. A newly graduated student from your school surprises you with a phone call to share the story of her first day as a graphic designer in an advertising company. She says, "The atmosphere in the office is so much like my experiences in your classroom. We work on client-oriented projects as teams, and we are expected to be individually accountable for our performances. We even use the same software and hardware!"

Class projects respond to real community issues and needs. A group of tenth graders present their proposal to the city's environmental com-

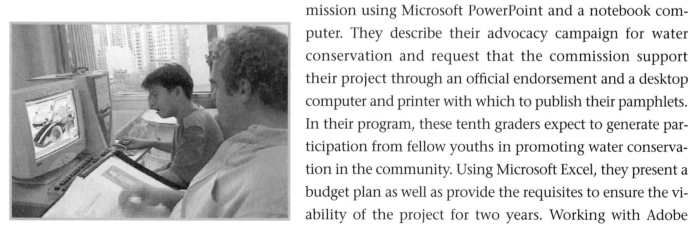

mission using Microsoft PowerPoint and a notebook computer. They describe their advocacy campaign for water conservation and request that the commission support their project through an official endorsement and a desktop computer and printer with which to publish their pamphlets. In their program, these tenth graders expect to generate participation from fellow youths in promoting water conservation in the community. Using Microsoft Excel, they present a budget plan as well as provide the requisites to ensure the viability of the project for two years. Working with Adobe

Photoshop, a digital camera, and a flatbed scanner, the group designs their own logo and creates the poster and pamphlets for their campaign.

Students are entrepreneurs. A team of sixth graders prepares flyers to announce the sale of holiday cards using Microsoft Word as the software for formulating text and Adobe Photoshop to create the graphics and layout design. The project was the culmination of their study of poetry genres. Unlike traditional poetry classes, students learned to write with an audience in mind and to use desktop publishing to publish their literary pieces. And so, based on a market study supported by information from the web, they realize the need to enhance their literary works to include visual media in a functional media art format, such as greeting cards. Students take pictures with a digital camera or draw them, then they scan their illustrations into Photoshop, where they are colorized. Finally, the cards are printed on a heavy card stock using an inkjet printer to fill orders from sales to parents, neighbors, relatives, and friends.

What Is So Unique About the Digital Generation?

I hate software manuals. When I look for one tool, it tells me to go to page this and that ... So I get to page 365 ... 30 minutes later ... I still can't find the instructions I need! If I write a manual on Adobe Photoshop, I'll start with the command called History. With this tool, I know exactly what I did. And most importantly I know I can make mistakes by un-clicking the commands I previously used. With History, I can tell my manual readers that I can undo my mistakes. It's a digital graphic artist's survival tool. —Amyel Oliveros, age 11

The Digital Generation

So, for the first time, there are things that parents want to be able to know about and do, where the kids are, in fact, the authority.

—John Seely Brown, Chief Scientist, Xerox PARC

Today's students are media savvy and restless. They crave connection, having an incessant desire to communicate and to nurture social relationships. They are also mostly bored with school and unable to relate

their education to their lives.

These students grew up with and depend on the web as if it were their best friend. It has become their intimate link to the peer network they passionately seek.

These young techies learn and tamper with software and hardware, pushing limits to the extreme, quickly and easily. Their intuitive relationship with technology will revolutionize learning in schools.

Moreover, true to its designation as the great equalizer, new communication and information technologies will offer this young generation the unprecedented opportunity to become major players in the use and evolution of digital media.

The illiterate of the 21st century will not be those who cannot read and write, but those who cannot learn, unlearn and relearn.
—*Alvin Toffler,*
Future Shock

Helical Learning: A 21st Century Learning Paradigm

Integrated Learning Strategy

Educational excellence is best achieved when students learn as authors, publishers, designers, inventors, teachers and entrepreneurs. Educated as if they were professional leaders, students take greater accountability for their learning.

This proactive environment nurtures students to achieve higher levels of comprehension through reason and mastery of subject matter. This they accomplish more effectively with hands-on projects predicated on analytical and imaginative applications.

The dynamic learning process is enhanced through an integrated learning strategy defined by three vital components: creative pedagogy, digital media technology, and peer-to-peer learning.

Creative pedagogy is a way of teaching that cultivates critical insight and use of imagination. It kindles analysis and invention. It enables students to transform knowledge toward real world projects where they in turn distill theories and formulate conclusions about the subject matter.

Digital media technology is hardware and software that encodes, stores, distributes, and produces interactive digital content. This includes audio, still images, video, animation, graphics, and data in a non-linear environment.

Digital media is a learner's tool that stimulates conceptualization and development of professionally-oriented projects.

Peer-to-peer learning is a participatory learning environment where students take on active roles in exploring, discovering, and building knowledge with peers, guided by adult teachers. It is a learning process that recognizes that when students teach each other and work together on projects, they have more fun. They produce more. They learn more.

With access to creative technology tools, students are challenged to solve problems and prepare presentations as a team of capable and supportive techno-savvy peers.

The Learning Helix

The Learning Helix is a process akin to inventive learning blocks. It engages students in a series of activities that build on each other. Starting with simple, fun lessons to build interest, the methodology provides students with hands-on activities to explore the subject matter. The process progresses to increasingly complex and imaginative tasks and culminates in an inventive project.

The Learning Helix has four levels. These are play, explore, integrate, and imagine.

Play: break the ice and introduce the topic. The subject matter is introduced through a fun interactive activity. Aware that most students enter classrooms with half their consciousness still absorbed by wherever they just came from, the teacher's goal is to arouse students' in-

For the last century, maps and compasses have been standard tools for most boys. Last year Morse's system of electronic signaling was eliminated from all maritime training and replaced by the Internet, wireless devices, and radio, satellite, and cellular telephones.

—Joseph A. Engelbrecht Jr., "A Future for Mapping: Mapping the Future" Imaging Notes, September/October 2001

In the fields of observation, chance favors only the prepared mind.
—*Louis Pasteur*

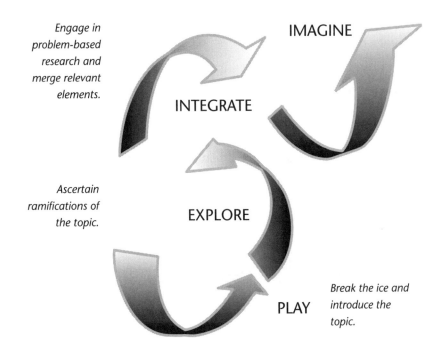

Engage in problem-based research and merge relevant elements.

IMAGINE

INTEGRATE

Ascertain ramifications of the topic.

EXPLORE

Break the ice and introduce the topic.

PLAY

terest. They address attitudes common in the first 10 minutes of class, which may include shyness, hyperactivity, whining, and a lack of focus. This first level assesses what students already know about the topic and focuses their attention to the current topic.

Explore: ascertain ramifications of the topic. Students discover, investigate, and find out more about the critical aspects of the topic with hands-on activities in small groups. The teacher harnesses their interests by giving them challenging problems to solve or questions that require research, discussion, and tangible outputs. They are also provided with hardware and software to expand their intelligences.

Integrate: merge and add content, technology applications and organization. Students engage in an increasingly complex activity where they need to access more information about the topic, defend their conclusions, and engage in work that requires leadership and cooperation.

Imagine: formulate innovative and viable alternatives. Students distill information from their research and transform their knowledge to respond to a need either in their communities, other target markets, or families. The solutions they create may be in the form of business or community project propositions. This is the most critical aspect of Helical Learning, because it is crucial that students see the value of knowledge as applied to real needs in one's life and community. Moreover, the project should be able to raise students' awareness of their role as vital contributors to change and growth in their communities, locally, nationally, and globally.

Insights: Creating Theories

You need to distill juice from the pulp to taste the essence of the fruit.

Armed with issues and successes from interactive learning activities and class projects, as well as mastery of software and hardware, students can derive relevant lessons about the topic. There is a fundamental difference between learning in a traditional classroom and learning with the Helical Learning strategy. In the former, the teacher is the chief source of knowledge. In the latter, it is the students' collective experience that becomes the critical and primary source of knowledge. The teacher facilitates theorizing using guidelines defined by goals anchored to real issues and education standards and adapted to students' learning styles and abilities. The students, enthused by the collective experiences they went through and with access to new and relevant information, cooperatively distill knowledge about the subject matter and generate conclusions and solutions.

For example, when a student first writes poetry without being given all the rules of writing, she or he will struggle with word usages, language structure, and creative techniques. This valuable experience will provide her with insights that will stimulate her participation, let's say, in a literary criticism class on poetry genres. When a student plays an interactive learning game that involves role-playing scenarios featuring court hearings on civil rights, he or she will have simulated experiences of success and failure to spawn lessons about the topic. Participatory experiences provide students with the emotional and cognitive foundations to actively and intelligently draw upon their own theories about any topic.

Moreover, with the real-world projects made possible by digital media, students will get feedback not only from the class, but also from their community partners. Desktop publishing and digital movies expand their audiences.

Theorizing begins with random feedback about the activity that has just taken place. The teacher asks questions that trigger positive and negative reactions from students, leading to more questions that segue into a critical discussion. The students distill juice from the pulp by articulating lessons from their experiences. Students develop their own theories and are able to correlate their experiences and conclusions with concepts in their books.

Working With Windows and Mac Systems

This book offers creative solutions for software that can be used for both Mac and PC systems, including Microsoft Office, Adobe Photoshop and Macromedia Dreamweaver, as well as programs that can be used in only one or the other, for example, iMovie for Mac and VideoStudio for the PC.

The operating system (OS) is like the engine that runs the car. It is important that you determine what type of OS your computer has in order to efficiently run the software recommended in this book.

The PC-Windows OS

Windows

Windows is used by more than 90 percent of desktop computers. This book will refer primarily to Windows XP, which is the latest Windows version, though this should not limit readers using Windows 95, Windows ME, or Windows 2000. If you are using Windows ME, you might consider saving up for Windows XP, because XP provides a much more expandable capability for multiprocessor systems and is able to support more users and bigger applications and files, as well as the demanding memory requirements of newer programs.

Located at the bottom of your screen
is the START key. Click to open a program or file.

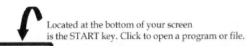

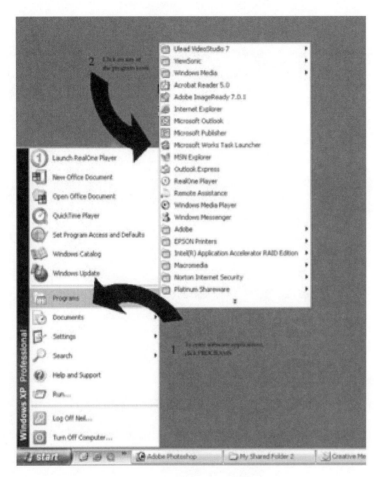

To open a program, click and hold the Start button and choose Programs. A list of programs will be shown in a menu.

You can open multiple documents and
programs at any one time.

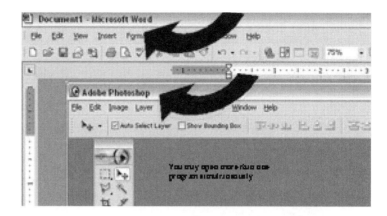

Save

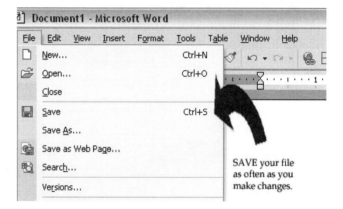

Shutdown

Mac OS

While Apple computers are less widespread, the company's role as a pioneer in the development of the graphical user interface (GUI) is key to the evolution of user-friendly systems. Unlike the PC, the Mac OS is made by the same company that makes the hardware, which means that users are less likely to find compatibility issues between the OS and the hardware. This book will refer primarily to Mac OS X, which is the latest version. However, this should not prevent readers from using OS 9 for the activities provided in this book.

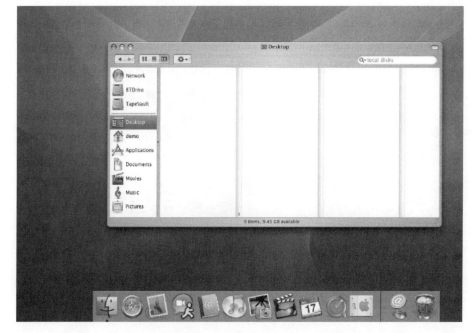

The Mac OS

Finding applications

Using a variety of software

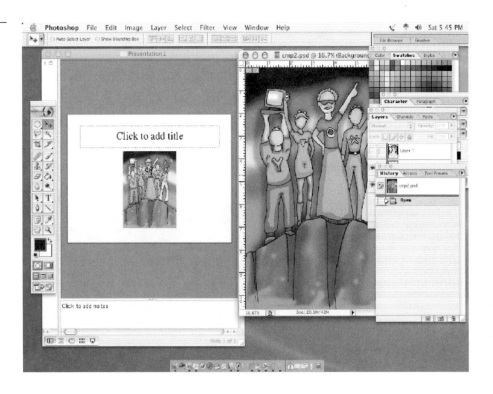

Apple finder

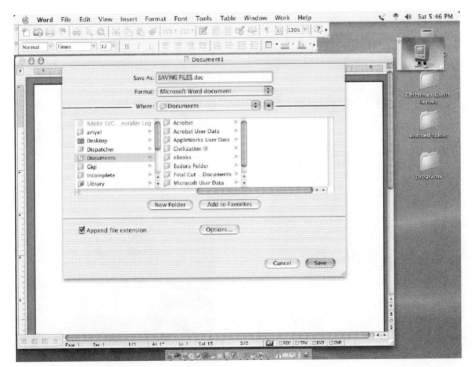

Saving files

Cross-Platform Software

A platform refers to an operating system. Cross-platform software refers to computer programs designed to function on both Mac and PC systems. In this book you will find activities and projects using Adobe Photoshop Elements, Microsoft Word, Microsoft PowerPoint, and Macromedia Dreamweaver. These software programs are available in most schools.

In most exercises, you will note how steps jump from one application to another. Digital media becomes even more useful for teaching content, as software tools are designed increasingly for compatability. An example of an activity is the Purple Frog, where the process of teaching students to write poetry expands from writing text and keyboarding to the use of imagery to stimulate writing and create a multimedia presentation.

Note that both iMovie and VideoStudio also use other programs to enhance text and images. Most of the activities require users to import and export images, audio, and text between applications.

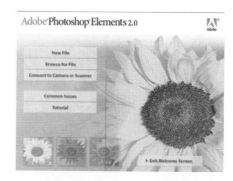

Photoshop and Photoshop Elements

All the graphics exercises in this book can be implemented with either Photoshop or Photoshop Elements. While Photoshop is considered the industry standard for image editing, Photoshop Elements, designed for less savvy users, has about the same capabilities. Photoshop CS, the latest version, is used as the primary software for graphics exercises. Where there is a big difference in interface between these two software systems, its equivalent in Photoshop Elements will be provided. You need not worry if you have the earlier versions of Photoshop or Photoshop Elements, you will still be able to use the exercises.

Among all the software introduced here, Photoshop and Photoshop Elements will have the steepest learning curves. Quite a number of teachers learning this software for the first time are frustrated with the tools. However, constant use will pay off, providing you with new ways to communicate concepts, insights, feelings, and dialogues in visual imagery. What is important to remember is that non-artists will be able to achieve phenomenal ways to visually communicate even the most complex concepts.

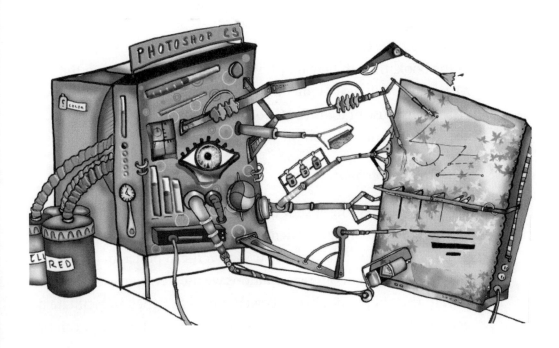

Don't worry about being thoroughly familiar with the software. When you teach the basics of any software to students, they will tend to take it to the next level on their own. This ability can be used to everyone's advantage. Encourage the more advanced students to help their classmates with the activities, freeing you to focus on teaching content.

For more information on Photoshop and Photoshop Elements, see www.adobe.com.

Microsoft Word

Writing activities will encourage students to explore Word's tools to stimulate writing. Word has expanded from a writing tool to a limited publishing tool. The latest version provides users with tools for bringing in photographs and images from other software and creating graphic organizers.

With Word's language-support tools, activities may also be used in teaching foreign languages. Editing and review tools are introduced as students collectively engage in publishing magazines, newspapers, and other media. Exercises in Word help students expand their vocabulary and improve their grammar.

If you have earlier versions of Word, you may still use the exercises in the book, though here may be a few tools not available in the non-XP versions. Whatever limitations the older versions may have may be offset by the use of tools in Microsoft PowerPoint.

For more information on Word, see www.microsoft.com.

Microsoft PowerPoint

Remember the carousel slideshow that took forever to produce and cost so much to prepare? Microsoft PowerPoint offers an alternative.

Many schools today are still using overhead projectors. Each time we make changes in our presentations we use new transparencies and discard the old plastic sheets. PowerPoint is designed to facilitate paperless production of dynamic multimedia presentations. It can produce the digital equivalent of a combined carousel slide show, an overhead projector topped with video and music.

PowerPoint is used to develop ideas for storyboarding; creating pictures; animating poetic images; illustrating literary stories, scientific discussions, and historical narratives; and supporting oral reports.

PowerPoint's flexibility and fluidity combined with its image tools also makes it possible for teachers to design their own graphic organizers, specific to lesson requirements.

Unlike the slide and the overhead projectors, PowerPoint can kill two birds with one stone. The presentation document can also be used to produce the paper counterpart.

For more information on PowerPoint, see www.microsoft.com.

Macromedia Dreamweaver

Dreamweaver gives teachers a much more visual approach to creating virtual classrooms. A few years ago, one could not imagine creating a web site without mastering HTML and other technologies such as JavaScript.

With Dreamweaver MX, the latest version, you need not know code to produce a highly attractive and efficient virtual on-line classroom. With proper planning, organization of text and images, and use of attractive graphics elements, it will take you less than three days to put together the first version of a five-page web site.

See www.macromedia.com for information on Dreamweaver.

Dreamweaver

Single-Platform Software

Moviemaking is such a dynamic and phenomenally engaging classroom project. You will be constantly amazed at what students are able to produce and learn with the use of desktop video editing software and the digital camera.

About 10 years ago, when analog was the format for video, creating movies was the turf of professional cameramen and editors. Recognizing the ability of movies to enhance education delivery, classrooms were equipped with VHS systems and large-screen televisions. In most classes, movies were used as a springboard for discussions. While movies and documentaries provide classrooms with an enriched experience, teachers are limited to existing movies and documentaries, which are not necessarily designed for courses.

Teaching moviemaking in classes such as math, history, science, and language arts requires an editing software that does not overshadow the learning of subject matter. A movie project could be a positive experience for students as it offers multiple learning goals and addresses multiple learning styles. Students are engaged in professional skills that involve interpretation of subject matter, technical competency, creative insight, and managing organizational structure and process. However, it could be counter-productive for academically-oriented classes if students get bogged down in the complexities of the editing software or hardware incompatibilities.

The desire to stress content over technology guided my choice of two applications—iMovie for the Mac and VideoStudio for the PC. These are entry-level, yet they have powerful tools that are easy to learn and compelling for enhanced classroom learning. Middle and high school students usually take 30 minutes to learn the interface and two to three hours to edit a simple three-minute movie.

Ulead VideoStudio

The interface of VideoStudio offers intuitive drag-and-drop capabilities to cut and paste images into an editor's movie timeline. VideoStudio can accommodate a broad variety of still and moving images. Students are able to organize these images into a logical order with the timeline.

The software provides users with hundreds of special effects such as transitions, overlay, and text tools. These special effects significantly contribute to the quality and overall clarity of message for content-oriented movies.

VideoStudio 8

The final project may be output in various media. These include DVD, VCD, or SVCD, as well as streaming web video or as an e-mail attachment.

Much to the chagrin of budget officers, video-editing software requires additional parts for your hardware. You need to look into the size and speed of your hard drive, RAM, and processor. The good news is that the cost of hardware, such as memory and RAM, have become less expensive in the past few years. Video Studio also requires a firewire cable to capture movie clips from the DV camera to its interface. The minimum hardware setup on the PC is:

- Windows 98 SE, ME, 2000, or XP
- Intel Pentium III 800MHz CPU
- 256MB of RAM, preferably 512MB
- 600 MB of available hard disk space, 4GB recommended
- 30GB Ultra-DMA/66 7200 rpm hard drive
- Video for Windows and DirectShow-compatible video capture card
- Windows-compatible sound card
- CD-ROM or DVD-ROM drive

For more information on VideoStudio, see www.videoStudio.com.

Apple iMovie

iMovie is bundled with Mac systems. If you want to purchase the most recent version, you can do so through the Mac web site.

iMovie can import music from iTunes and still images from iPhoto. This allows students to focus on editing. For example, when you want students to create a movie about a scientific experiment they conducted in class and structure this according to "Before, During and After," you will want them to be able to make sense of the information they gather from many sources, including the web, printed materials, scanned images, photographs, and digital video.

It is very helpful to learn the iLife package. iMovie 4 provides

Apple iMovie

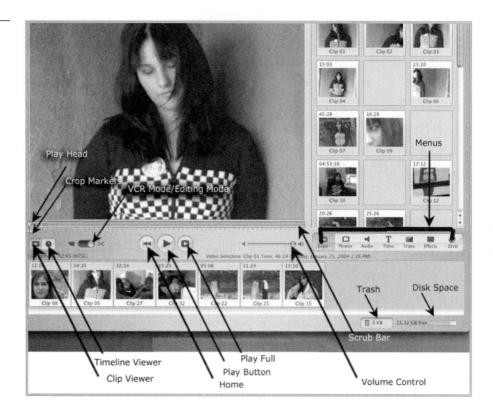

visual effects, which includes Letterbox, Electricity, Flare, and Aged Film. You can trim video and audio clips directly in the timeline.

You can align audio and video clips using the alignment tools as well as lock your final edit using the lock audio clip at Playhead option in the Advanced Menu and keep these secured as you work on the rest of your movie.

iMovie has easy-to-manipulate stretchable handles, found along the timeline, to adjust visual and audio effects. The Ken Burns Pan and Zoom effect lets you create powerful, professional imagery with stills.

iMovie allows you to have three audio tracks. Users may combine tracks to highlight emotional scenes, dialogue, and still images. Editing voice narration has never been so easy.

For more information on iMovie, see www.apple.com.

The World Wide Web

One of the best gifts for a teacher is easy access to multimedia information, which was an unthinkable possibility before the 1990s. I must say, the web is my best friend when I need information, ideas, and images to keep my students excited. This is probably why more than 90 percent of all U.S. schools are connected to the web. It is an invaluable source of information.

The web has grown rapidly, along with various technologies, to accommodate moving images, such as Flash, Java applets, and MPEG video. Many students are familiar with ways to download their favorite tunes from the web as well as with various file formats.

The web will be a constant resource for activities, primarily to engage students in research and to open their minds to the vast universe of information. Equal access to the web becomes a key factor in the necessary shift of knowledge and power in the classroom.

Netscape

Internet Explorer

Digital Hardware Accessories

Along with software, teachers need to familiarize themselves with accessories such as the digital camera, digital video (DV) camera, scanner, printer, memory cards, and cables. These tools are all part of the digital learning environment.

Digital Camera

A digital camera provides learners with a powerful tool that captures images to demonstrate evidence of theoretical ideas. It is an empowering tool that students can use for presentations, publications, art projects, and web sites. Digital pictures record scientific experiments, people in action, places, events, changes in the environment, sports, games, drama presentations, dances, or storyboards. Since images are already digitized, there is no need for scanning.

Find the highest resolution at the lowest cost. Resolution is expressed in megapixels, or the number of squares that compose the

Digital camera

Digital camera

image. The higher the number, the sharper the picture appears. If you intend to print a photograph at 8.5 x 11 inches, a 3.0 megapixel camera is good. However, if you have a bigger budget, consider getting one with higher resolution.

Look for faster shutter response speed. Lower-end cameras tend to have slow shutter response speeds. This means you wait for a while before you can take the next shot.

Other useful features include zoom abd wide lenses, manual and automatic control modes, and interchangeable lenses and flash attachments.

Digital video camera.

FireWire

Flatbed scanner

Digital Video Camera

Digital video (DV) cameras provide students with extraordinary ways to have a moving "visual" voice. Shooting with digital video cameras is relatively inexpensive compared with analog cameras. Film, when used more than once, causes image quality to degenerate. On the other hand, digital videotapes can be used multiple times without image degeneration.

The best combination of quality and price are DV cameras on the prosumer level. These models include some of the more important components of professional cameras for a third of the price. Today's DV cameras come with an LCD monitor. Make sure it has a FireWire connection for video and an USB connection for photos. Look for the highest resolution. A full set of manual options and auto-exposure effects provide greater flexibility. Low-light sensitivity allows you to shoot in poorly lit environments. Zoom lenses can help you create in higher quality images using a variety of techniques.

Flatbed Scanner

Projects that require digitizing photographs, illustrations, signatures, documents, and flat objects are best done with a flatbed scanner. The illustrations in this book were drawn by hand, inked with pen, and digitized with a flatbed scanner. Thereafter, as a digital image, Amyel used Photoshop to digitally paint and enhance the lines of his drawings.

Look for the ability to scan at 2400 pixels per inch (ppi). Optical character recognition (OCR) allows the scanner to read text documents as characters, which offers a more efficient way to digitize documents, rather than typing. Being able to scan at a minimum of 25 seconds per page hastens the process. Better software allows you to scan directly to a file format of your choice. It should also provide for separate tools for scanning black-and-white and colored materials.

Printer

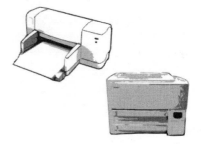

Inkjet and laser printers

With high-quality printouts you will be able to transform your classroom into a publishing center. With the three-year-old inkjet in the high school where I worked, my students were able to produce remarkable postcards, greeting cards, bookmarks, magazines, flyers, anthologies of short stories, and poetry.

Being able to publish and distribute art and literary works is an incredible experience for students. Printers help expand the audiences of student writers and artists. Having more people appreciate students' works makes it more exciting and challenging for students on the one hand, yet on the other hand, it is the acknowledgement of the real world, the writer's audience that brings about true confidence in their abilities.

There are two general types of digital printers: inkjet and laser. Laser printers are less costly in the long run because they don't consume as much ink as inkjets printers, but they are more expensive. There are two types of laser printers—full color and black and white.

In buying inkjet printers, look for low-cost ink cartridges, a minimum speed of 18 pages per minute, a minimum resolution of 4800 X 1200 dpi (dots per inch) and the ability to print in color and black-and-white.

Memory card

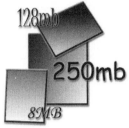

External Memory Card

Computers crash. I'm always ready with some kind of a backup option to make sure that if the hardware breaks down, the files students have worked so hard will remain intact. This is critical, especially with complex projects such as movies and publications.

One of my co-teachers at the Digital Media Academy came by my classroom last summer with a very high-tech looking necklace. She explained, "It's the extension of my hard drive." I found out then that her pendant could also be used as a key chain.

The hard drive she was wearing is called a USB flash drive. You insert the drive into the USB slot on your computer, and the drive will appear on your desktop, where you can drag and save your files.

Cables

FireWire **USB** Audio/Video Cables

Cables

There are several types of cables to complete your basic digital classroom set-up. These include the (1) Firewire, (2) USB, and (3) audio/video cables. Both the USB and Firewire drivers allow computers to immediately identify the gadget and automatically apply the appropriate drivers.

Firewire cable—use to connect DV cameras to CPUs for uploading and downloading of movie images.

USB cable—use to connect digital cameras, digital microscopes, MPEG, and CD Players to computers.

Video/audio cables—use to connect the camera and television to VCR, DVD, and Laser Disk systems.

2

The Digital Generation and the Rapidly Changing World

■ How many times have we heard our students complain, "This class is boring!" And then ... ?

Learning Language With Technology

I once taught English as a Second Language in a high school in California. During the first few months of classes, my students could hardly speak an English sentence without stopping to think of the next word or to combine words from their first language. It was always a challenge to ask them to express their thoughts and feelings. I commonly heard, "Me no speak English good." Confident that they were going to learn English, I'd respond by saying, "That's okay, you will do so very soon." About a third of my students were gang members whose minds were often preoccupied by their gang activities. Many of my students had been living here for less than three years and most had hardly been able to adjust to the way of life in the U.S.

aving worked with tech-savvy teenagers in a third-world country and seen students facing complex challenges as immigrants to the U.S., I decided to create a learning environment that was fun, interactive, and effective at preparing them to succeed as professionals in the 21st century. I engaged my teens in learning the English language through digital media projects.

Every Thursday we had long class periods, about one and a half hours. That was enough time for me to get the students working in the computer lab.

In the beginning of the school year, not one of the students had any significant experience with computers and the software we were using. In a sense, this was good because their technology skills were on an equal level, and I was not worried about their abilities and interests in learning technology.

Movement and Word Meanings

Recognizing the variety of learning styles described in *Multiple Intelligences* by Howard Gardner and the different educational backgrounds of students in the class, I ventured to create activities that made use of visual-spatial, kinesthetic, intra-personal, inter-personal, and verbal-linguistic abilities of the students.

I introduced students to three verbs: click, press, and move. Any software provided immediate response to their actions (kinesthetic and visual), and this helped them to remember the meanings of the words.

As we opened Microsoft Word, I used these verbs repeatedly in my oral instructions. I used an LCD projector to illustrate what the words meant as I moved the mouse. Most of the students followed accordingly. I watched their monitors and their faces and saw their fascination; technology clearly played a key role in keeping them engrossed in the activity. I introduced nouns and simple instructional sentences related to these three words, such as click the button, press the key, and move the mouse. I made the students repeat after me when I used the phrases in my instructions. I wanted them to remember the sounds of these words as they performed their steps.

A few students were initially intimidated by the workstations and probably unsure whether they understood my instructions. To enable me to address individual needs in a fun and engaging way, I instructed the rest of the class to type their names using Word's Word Art tool. Typing their names and playing with the creative possibilities of the tool captivated students. In fact, if left on their own, they would play with this tool for the entire hour and a half. While most of the students' eyes are glued to their monitors with this activity, I worked with those who needed one-on-one support.

With students who were afraid of the computer, I held the mouse and asked each one to place his or her hand on top of mine. I wanted them to feel the motion of my hand in response to instructions (kinesthetic). I deleted whatever we did and asked them to repeat the words and the action we did together, this time on their own. I watched as they worked out the correlation between their actions and the words and found their own way to manipulate the software. When there were too many students asking for help, I asked the more tech-savvy individuals to help their peers.

The students were very excited about learning software. In the next meeting, they asked me to teach them how to create email accounts. During lunch and after school, I noticed that at least one third of them were practicing our lessons and emailing their friends in the lab.

In the next two weeks, they wrote and edited poems with Word. They learned new words each time they learned a new command, and I instructed them to use grammar and vocabulary tools to enhance their writings. After three weeks, students produced anthologies of original love poems. They learned how elements of poetry writing enabled them to creatively communicate ideas and feelings. Using graphics and layout tools in Word, they published their anthologies, made copies on a photocopier, and distributed them to their parents and peers. I doubt

that my students would have learned English this fast or this enthusiastically had we not used computers combined with fun and engaging writing activities.

Technology and Meaningful Learning

By the end of the first quarter, the students had published their first English narratives about their childhood, which we called "Childhood and Dreams." The anthology reflects the aspirations of immigrant families from the perspectives of children. The work also mirrored students' feelings about their social, physical, and cultural environments, an evolving pattern of immigrant life in the U.S. They never complained about being bored in class. They enjoyed seeing their thoughts and feelings manifested on screen. By the end of the first semester, they proudly published their fantasy stories, which were based on Mayan and Aztec mythology.

To these students, learning English was the result of learning digital technology and desktop publishing. Learning software, authoring, publishing, and selling their works convinced the students that learning English provided them with a new skill and a way to earn money from their talents. They were fascinated and empowered as they learned. Throughout the year, these students also learned how to conduct research on the web, write and edit using Word, and create multimedia presentations using PowerPoint. Isn't it amazing how the combination of appropriate technology and creative pedagogy allows students to learn so much and love learning in a relatively short period of time?

Technology Enthuses Learners

Each time we had class, the students were on an emotional high. Except for one or two distracted students, each of them enthusiastically explored software while mastering the subject matter and the English language in their poems, narratives, and myths. Psychologists Mihaly Csikszentmihalyi and Ellen Langer have termed this state optimum flow. It occurs when students achieve higher learning goals because learning matters to them. "Alienation gives way to involvement, enjoyment replaces boredom, helplessness turns into a feeling of self-control, and psychic energy works to reinforce the sense of self, instead of being lost in the service of external goals" (Mihaly Csikszentmihalyi, *Flow: The Psychology of Optimal Experience* [New York: Harper and Row, 1990], 69).

What Is the Digital Generation?

Dubbed by marketers as Generation Y, the digital generation includes every K–12 child who has access to a digital tool. The digital generation includes children who learned to use the VCR at the age of two and began playing computer games at the age of three. With the flooding of multimedia gadgets and accessories in the marketplace, this generation has redefined the concept of multitasking. They can hardly work on their assignments without a portable CD player while interacting with their friends in virtual chatrooms.

Generation Y, or the "Millenials" as they prefer to be called, are the children of the Boomers and early-wave members of Generation X. Accounting for 27% of America's population, they are 70 million strong. Born between 1982 and 2000, this first generation of the new millennium populates classes in elementary, middle, and high schools, as well as undergraduate and graduate programs at colleges and universities (Achievement for All Children, An Apple Perspective, www.apple.com.)

Unlike past generations, these learners are flooded with media options—television, radio, CD players, cell phones, computer and video games, chat rooms, email, and Internet sites.

In 1998, Don Tapscott wrote *Growing Up Digital*. He underscored the impact of technology in our society and how the Net Generation, which is equivalent to Generation Y, will require a more tech-oriented and dynamic learning environment. "The Net Generation children using GlobaLearn are beginning to process information and learn differently than the boomers before them. New media tools offer great

promise for a new model of learning—one based on discovery and participation. This combination of a new generation and new digital tools will cause a rethinking of the nature of education—in both content and delivery" (Tapscott, *Growing Up Digital* New York: McGraw-Hill, 1998, 127).

Yet many of these students feel empty within. They find no excitement in discovery and expanding their imaginations. Something about the kind of world they are exposed to drives them to depression and indifference to issues that matter to their health, happiness, and success. They search for meaning in the most unrealistic fashion. I have had to counsel quite a few of my high school students about not physically hurting themselves, for example, in gang confrontations or slashing their wrists.

While media has been increasingly competing for the large sums of money in the teen market, these students need more attention than we can imagine. There is a pervasive feeling of isolation. Many have lost their wonder about life and are negative about opportunities provided to them. In addition to teaching them content, if we fail to recognize and address these issues, our students will be unable to connect education with a sense of empowerment, self-fulfillment, and joy. When they do not enjoy learning, education to these young digital geniuses is boring.

Technology Fuels Change

I am one of many in the current generation of teachers who did not have a clue as to how the Internet and computers would alter the delivery of education.

Technology is accelerating change at an even more rapid pace than it did 10 years ago. To make it even more unsettling, our children's perception of the world today will not be the same five to ten years from now. If many of us could not have fathomed how technology has transformed business, medicine, scientific research, communications, and distribution, in a very short period of time, how can our students envision the future? With the way technology is changing the way the world works, how will our students survive the future? What kind of education do we provide them to ensure their future successes? Is the pace and degree of change contributing to our students' anxieties and depression?

Physiological and psychological studies reveal how the digital generation's learning processes are affected by their early exposure to digital media and the web. They are so at ease with software and fascinated by electronic devices, much more so than we adult teachers are.

Success and Learning Fundamentals

Have the fundamentals about professional success changed?

While on the one hand digital media facilitates meaningful, critical, and project-based learning, technology also has the ability to control and negatively affect its users. Arming students with a working knowledge of software and hardware architecture will allow them to be in better control of the manipulative nature of digital media.

In a *Fortune* magazine article about Bill Gates, the founder of Microsoft, Brent Schlender explains how Longhorn, the next-generation Windows operating system will influence all of our lives in the very near future, "Your PC will keep track of how you work, whom you talk to, what sites you look at, how you make documents and whom you share them with, which data on the network are yours—making all those things easier" (*Fortune*, July 8, 2002, 64).

Computer operating systems are designed to meet people's everyday needs and will inevitably make us ever more dependent on them. Computer companies will continue to spend billions of dollars on research and development to find more ways to allow technology to further penetrate the way we work and live.

The structure of software will affect the way we think and learn. In his book *Being Digital*, Nicolas Negroponte, the founder of the MIT

Media Lab, compares atoms and bits, saying that atoms are reminiscent of the past framework of human thought processes and bits are the new digital and non-linear (human) way of processing information. According to Negroponte, "The global information highway is about the global movement of weightless bits at the speed of light ... that future is driven almost 100% by the ability of that company's product or services to be rendered in digital form" (*Being Digital* New York: Vintage, 1996).

Thinking in bits instead of atoms means transforming mental frameworks from linear to non-linear and from passive to interactive. In the 1980s, televisions were set up in classrooms to enhance learning, but today television is considered passive media.

We need to address the learning issues of our Millenial students to prepare them for an increasingly digital world. Our students will not be bored if they are inspired, empowered, and enjoying learning.

Education can be effective only if it touches our students' sensibilities and if they can see what good it offers, not solely based on what adults think, but on their ability to communicate their unique perceptions. They need to be able to see language in action. They need to be able to transform media that has numbed them into a medium of empowerment—as a way to project their voices. They need to know that their needs and views matter.

In 1991, the Labor Department, through the Secretary's Commission on Achieving Necessary Skills, published a report, *What Work Requires of Schools*, that underscored the importance of competence, and knowledge, and such skills as listening and speaking, problem solving, creative thinking, knowing how to learn, collaboration, and organizational effectiveness. Learning technology empowers students to perform in professionally oriented environments and empowers them only if pedagogy challenges them in these areas.

I liken this learning environment to Joseph Campbell's description in *Myth and the Modern World*: "People say that what we're all seeking a meaning for life.... The experience of being alive...." He says myths are valuable to every generation "so that our life experiences on the purely physical plane will have resonances within our innermost being and reality ... so that we actually feel the rapture of being alive" (Joseph Campbell, *The Power of Myth).*

■ Students report feeling bored, unmotivated, or simply forgotten. Nearly 450,000 youth drop out of school each year and do not return. —YouthBuild USA **www.youthbuild.org** (Feb. 26, 2003)

■ Nearly one-third of American students aren't graduating high school. This represents nothing short of massive failure of America's high schools. —Tom Vander Ark, Executive Director of Education for the Bill & Melinda Gates Foundation (*Educational Leadership*, Vol. 59 No. 5, February 2002, 55–59)

Picture the traditional classroom. Each student sits at a desk. The desks are arranged in rows facing the board. The teacher lectures about a topic or asks students to read a literary piece with him. Then the teacher distributes activity sheets to each student and instructs them to answer questions and fill the blanks. The students work individually on their desks and submit their papers to the teacher. The bell rings and the class is dismissed.

In another classroom, the teacher assigns an essay about some readings. In broad strokes, she discusses the structure of the paper, for example, a five-paragraph essay. Some of the students grumble. The

Writing essays sucks! The assignment is way too long and tedius.

So tell me, what is a topic sentence?

Writing English essays will help us get to the best universities.

teacher reminds them to read the next chapter for the next meeting. At the end of the lesson, the teacher measures how much the students have learned through a test.

Teachers in these types of traditional classrooms spend a significant amount of time *managing* their classes. Beneath the mantle of quietness on the one hand and restlessness on the other, many students are unable to make sense of the subject matter. Most complain of boredom. They are required to work on their own usually, and helping peers means sharing high grades, which is uncommon in this competitive educational culture.

While testing is quantifiable, I believe the more important aspect in education is preparing students for their future professions.

Traditional classroom environments are designed for the smaller percentage of students who are motivated to achieve high grades and who have made up their minds to pursue college degrees. However, most students are in school because their parents told them they have to be there, they crave socialization, and it is federal law. Given this context, it is imperative, therefore, that the learning environment addresses the majority of students who are not convinced that success in school is the basis of a bright future.

Empowering Learning Environments

A teacher's lesson plan and way of educating promotes a culture that pervades every aspect of learning. To create an empowering learning environment a teacher will need to take note of the needs, abilities, and goals of all students in the class. The lesson plan will need to address cognitive and emotional aspects of students, enabling them to effectively learn subject matter and to nurture professional and social skills.

The Helical Learning Strategy will motivate students by nurturing their talents and intelligences, cause students to discover their abilities with experiences that parallel what they will experience in professional learning environments, and offer them the opportunity to learn subjects they value and that impact their lives.

Learning and the Evolving Persona

Central to the Helical Learning strategy is the underlying goal of guiding students in defining their individual person. For learning to have true impact, it is critical that academic standards adapt to the student's sense of self. Classroom activities should be designed to grow the skills, knowledge, and emotional facets of the learners.

A proactive learning environment provides stimuli that engage students' core values. Inspiring, challenging, and fulfilling activities influence students' degree and rate of learning.

Helical Learning has three core elements: creative pedagogy, peer-to-peer learning, and cutting-edge technology.

Creative Pedagogy

Creative pedagogy stimulates critical insight and inventive thinking. It combines critical, innovative, and effective use of the elements of art as powerful tools addressing multiple intelligences in research, concept development, and communications projects.

It uses challenging and exciting activities based on the principles of aesthetic composition, which guide students in formulating creative, academic and project-based constructs for organizing information, ideas, and insights. Dynamic and fun interactive activities and projects engage students in research, review, problem-solving applications, and mastery of subject matter.

Sample Class: Interpreting a Sculpture

There are so many ways to introduce a topic. The first challenge is to seize students' hearts and minds and get them interested in the subject matter. Thereafter, to bring learning to a proactive and analytical level, the teacher will need to tap and cultivate students' critical in-

"Essentially, the aim of differential instruction is to maximize each student's growth by meeting each student where he or she is, helping the student to progress." (The Association for Supervisor and Curriculum Development, www.ascd.org, 2000.)

CREATIVE PEDAGOGY

sights and imaginations. This dynamic, engaged and meaningful process transforms students into proactive learners.

I will elucidate this concept further with an example of a beginning activity in research and writing.

The first activity establishes the bases and immediately provides students with a critical framework of the lesson. For this lesson plan, the introduction should demonstrate the importance of a writer's point of view in research and writing.

A standard approach is for the teacher to lecture on the concept. Another way is to read several short literary pieces and decipher the point of views in the materials. Both of these approaches will interest verbal-linguistic learning types and alienate the rest of the class. Most students pretend that they are working, yet their minds are anywhere but on the subject matter.

The beginning activity should stir the majority of students' interests in accomplishing a series of activities in the fields of reading, writing, and research. Specifically, I wanted to make sure that at the end of the activity, they understand and apply the concept of the writer's point of view and its implications in literary analysis, research, and writing.

Before the students arrived, I lined the tables and chairs by the walls and left one table at the center of the room. I instructed the students to hold onto their notebooks and pens and to sit on the floor, forming a circle around the table. I brought in a very unusual sculpture and placed it on the table. Then I divided the class into groups of three and asked each of the groups to write their descriptions of the sculpture, from where they sat. Some students complained, "I can't see anything!" I told them that it was impossible for them not to see anything because there was a sculpture right in front of their faces. More complained, "But I can't see it all!" I said that they may not see the entire sculpture, but that was all right. They were assigned to write whatever they saw. Finally they stopped complaining and wrote their observations.

I took the sculpture away. Each group shared their description. I asked the groups to write what they thought the sculpture was, based on what they perceived it to be; a group could have only one answer.

We moved to the computer lab, and I instructed members of groups to sit beside each other. I told them to go to www.google.com and type their answer to the question, "What is this sculpture?" For example, if a group thought the sculpture was an *African god*, they would type these two words in the information bar.

The students were instructed to click first the Images link and then enter their search term. The search resulted in a variety of images in each of their screens. Each group had to choose one, which, based on their interpretation, could have been the sculpture. I assured the class that there was no right or wrong in this activity. What was important was that their descriptions match their conclusions.

The teams clicked the image of their choice.

I instructed them to find out more about their image by going to its web site. To accomplish this, they needed to click on the link below the image.

In a gamelike activity, each of the teams was given one minute to list five important findings about the image from the web site. The first team that finished received five credits on their project grade. When all were done, they typed the information in paragraph form in a Word document. Each team member had to type one sentence at a time, while the rest contributed by making sure the paragraph made sense all the way. They had five minutes to accomplish the task. Once again, the first team that finished received five credits on their project grade.

I announced that I was going to play the role of a judge. "The court will please come to order! Everyone take your seats. I would like you to tell me, in the light of lack of evidence, what the stolen sculpture is!"

Each of the groups read their paragraph. There was amazement and laughter in the air about every different interpretation of the sculpture. Each group's point of view fascinated the rest. The students' spirits were elevated by the activity, and they were beginning to understand what was going on.

By reading their interpretation of the sculpture, students had something at stake in the activity. The atmosphere was positively competitive because all answers were correct. With a common experience about differing interpretations of the sculpture, the class was ready to reflect on the activity.

One student said different perspectives resulted in different research results and conclusions. Another added that it all depends on how we relate what we see to what we think it is from what we already know about the sculpture. The class kept citing examples of their findings as the discussion went on. They were formulating their own conclusions and relating these with their experiences.

With the students' clear articulations of the concept of point of view, all I needed to do was listen to their reflection and synthesize their findings with a statement at the end. I said, "That's what we mean by a writer's point of view," and then further explained the implications of point of view in research and literature.

I asked more details about the activity: What happened when you used Google to generate information about the image you described? What did you discover about search engines?

The exercise took about 30 minutes. It would not have taken this long if I had lectured on the topic, but it would not have achieved the same degree of critical understanding of the subject matter and level of engagement for the students.

This is creative pedagogy. It is a way of teaching and learning where emotional, physical, and mental faculties are engaged. This teaching makes students think outside the box, because they draw conclusions that are not meant to simply fill the blanks or fulfill the requirements as defined by the teacher in an essay, question-and-answer quiz, or activity sheets.

The activity involved students in the experience of creating knowledge. The focus was not what the teacher determined was right or wrong. The parameters were defined by the collective experience and the students' responses to the activities. The teacher provided students with a structured project-based activity and tools for critical analysis by asking insightful questions, where students actively formulated their conclusions.

The exercise above began with a radical change in the physical environment, with the informality of students sitting on the floor. In every step of the way, they were experiencing something unlike that of a traditional classroom. The sensation created by an informal environment provoked their unguarded responses. With a process that acknowledges what they see, students discover and begin to value their observation skills. As the teacher facilitates the theorization process, students recognize how responses to stimuli become bases for conclusions.

Technology kept students involved and helped them come up with higher quality paragraphs. The element of the unknown and immediate response mechanism provided by the search engine was critical in drawing students' attention to their project.

Addressing Multiple Intelligences

Creative pedagogy taps into your students' creative wellsprings to make them more aware of their innate intelligences. When nurtured through participation in projects, they realize how this becomes a powerful resource from which ideas and solutions emanate. Merged with technology, creative pedagogy provides stimuli through multiple media, for example, the sculpture as a visual object and the web browser interface. This pedagogy nurtures students' interests in knowledge acquisition by bringing to the fore the learners' various talents.

> The most recent research at Project Zero suggests that the arts may not directly improve performance in traditional academic subjects, but that the arts can help nurture an educational context in which students are more serious, more disciplined, more likely to take on new challenges, and more likely to value learning across the board.
> —John Gardner, "Concept to Classroom," notes from the
> online chat at www.disneylearningpartnership, January 2002

To enable the teacher to cultivate these various aptitudes, Helical Learning uses the elements of art and principles of composition as essential tools of a dynamic lesson plan.

Studies show that effective learning occurs when the pedagogy impacts the way we think, feel, and act. By using the elements of art and composition, we tap into our sensory abilities, which contributes to our learning. It allows students of various intelligences to express that which is subjective (feelings) and objective (concepts).

More important, the elements of art allow us to peer into the depths of our humanity, and through a reflective and research-oriented learning process connect this to a higher understanding of the world.

> We're so engaged in doing things to achieve purposes of outer value that we forget that the inner value, the rapture that is associated with being alive, is what it's all about.   —Joseph Campbell, *The Power of Myth*, 5

Sample Lesson: Learning About America

Following is a summarized version of an introductory lesson, applicable to any K–12 grade level.

Introductory Activity: Name Art

Instructions: Express your name creatively using PowerPoint's Word Art tool. Print each name. Link the first and last letters of each name with tape to form a circle of connected names.

There are several things students can get from this activity:

- The choices of font and colors reflect unique personalities.
- A circle of names connotes connectivity as in a web community.
- Rough textures reflect our imperfection as people.
- Individual identities are symbolized by names.
- Colors reflect various personalities and choices.

The activity acknowledges the students, highlights their individuality, and symbolizes the learning community of the classroom.

Subject Matter Application: Contemporary America

After focusing on their names, creating a sense of belonging to a learning community, participants share more about themselves in a free writing activity. They will learn how to edit grammar and vocabulary errors. Software: Microsoft Word.

Through a create-your-own-motif activity, the lesson will illustrate the diversity of students' backgrounds and cultures in the learning community. Software: web browser and Adobe Photoshop.

The students will put their biographies with the motifs. They will not sign their names. The motifs represent their identities.

The teacher introduces Word as desktop-publishing software. The students are guided in creating a one-page presentation integrating all the above activities. After printing, the teacher collects the papers and with the help of the class, posts each of the students' sheets to form the map of America.

The teacher concludes, "We are all part of America. The activities we accomplished highlight the multicultural landscape of the U.S. today."

Deconstructing the Lesson Plan

The lesson plan turns the classroom into a microcosm of America, the bigger context from which students nurture their sense of selves. By designing their own names with the Word Art tool, the learning culture here embraces diversity and individuality. Students are made to realize that by respecting their uniqueness, they will feel better about themselves.

Instead of just hearing about these concepts, students created them from their collective participation. Forming individual names in Word Art and connecting this in a circle defines the sense of the whole by the contribution of its parts. The very process and artistic expression is reflective of the evolving multicultural landscape of America.

To highlight content, students are introduced to three software systems, just like these were everyday tools to help them think imaginatively, brainstorm, organize their thoughts, and communicate their ideas.

The use of the elements of art and composition provides students with a variety of options to express their ideas. This is vital to bringing participation to higher, broader, and more dynamic levels of subject matter understanding.

The elements of art, which include line, shape, texture, color, rhythm, sound, and space are combined with elements of composition which include value, contrast, composition, balance, chronology, surprise, and more. This creates knowledge in sensory, multimedia, and concrete manners. For example, instead of just saying or writing the words "older generation," they may describe this concept in pictures and visual symbols or text that include wrinkled faces, dual-vision eyeglasses, typewriters, and more.

The elements of art and composition become expressive tools for descriptions and observations. They are a combination of visual, physical, musical, and cognitive guideposts for research activities. For example, instead of just making students write their observations in a science experiment, they will have a more holistic understanding, as they are made visually aware of the texture, color, and hue of a material before, during, and after adding a chemical solution. They can take pictures with a digital camera for accuracy in their presentation. Thereafter, to present possibilities of what could have been with variables, students will use graphic software to manipulate color, texture, and size. Invariably, their sense of color is enhanced by their hands-on experiences in digitally controlling hue in combination with other visual elements.

Furthermore, these creative elements present a visual representation of mental organization. Graphic organizers are very helpful in bringing out as many ideas as possible and connecting these ideas in a manner that makes sense. With moviemaking software, students have digital storyboards that visually represent the mental flow of their project. The interactive nature of software allows them to reorganize and manipulate elements of their digital movie projects in real time.

More important, the combined elements of art and composition provide students with expressive and potent tools to stimulate thinking about possibilities. This is Helical Learning.

Cutting-Edge Technology

Every kind of software is designed for multiple purposes. As teachers it will be very advantageous to have working knowledge of at least five types of software. By understanding the nature of software and the way these programs work together in a given operating system, teachers will be able to enhance the learning environment. The

CUTTING EDGE TECHNOLOGY

power of digital media in a learning environment lies in the mastery and creative integration of hardware, software, and content.

Digital media is hardware and software that encodes, stores, distributes, and produces digital content. It is non-linear technology designed to produce audio, still images, video, animation, graphics, and data.

Interactive media is a graphical user interface that enables users to interact with the computer. The quality and speed of interaction is determined by the processor speed, bandwidth, hardware, software code, and content.

Hardware consists of components of the computer that are physically handled. These include the microprocessors, commonly referred to as the brain of the computer.

Software is the code or instructions defined by a programming language. This code determines the interface and controls hardware.

Interactive Technology Is Magical

I observed a few classes in computer labs supervised by fellow teachers. In these classes the general pattern would be similar. First, the teacher warns students that they are prohibited from going to any interactive game sites. Then the teacher explains the research project each student will have to accomplish. As soon as the students hear the word "research," a few will turn to face their monitors and go to gaming sites.

The teacher continues with the explanation of the research paper requirements. A few students take notes of key points in the outline. A few students ask questions such as, "How many pages do you want? Is it double-spaced? How much time do we have to do the research paper?" Mostly, students are concerned about the mechanics.

No one asks what the research paper signifies as a learning project. Most students eagerly await the end of the teacher's explanation so they can begin online chatting, emailing, navigating through e-commerce sites and checking out the latest fashions—anything but the research assignment.

As soon as they see the teacher coming, students click the mouse to return to the web site where their teacher expects them to research the topic. With one click they get away with pretending to work in class.

Five days pass and most of the students have not done a thing for their research project. The teacher reminds them they have three days left before deadline. That seems like a long time. They continue to socialize, play, and shop online. The day before submission date, these students finally check out the web sites on the teacher's list.

They know how to copy and paste text in Word. If there are a few who don't, their friends teach them. They traverse five web sites, copying and pasting lines combining information from web pages into their Word document. They read through their two-page research papers and change some words in the sentences, so they can say, "These are our own words," and "We wrote this essay." They have no time to edit. They turn their papers in at the last minute.

Indeed, in this context interactive technology is magical. Without digging into the subject matter and instead copying information easily accessed through the web, these students are able to put together their research assignments in a maximum of two hours. Phenomenal!

The big question is, did they learn anything with technology integration in the curriculum? This example demonstrates how technology made it easier for them to pretend they were learning.

How can we even consider technology for schools if it fails to raise learning to a higher level?

Students' Perception of Technology

In his book *Growing Up Digital*, Don Tapscott aptly describes the Net Generation. "Today's kids are so bathed in bits that they think it's all part of the natural landscape. To them digital technology is no more intimidating than a VCR or toaster" (Tapscott, *Growing Up Digital* New York: McGraw-Hill, 1998).

Mostly, today's generation of students learn about new technologies through friends. They convince their parents to buy a computer for home use, so that they can get into online chatting, interactive gaming, and email. They download music and listen to their CD or MP3 players. Every day, there is a new facet to digital technology, be it a new web site, a new interactive game, or a new gadget.

Technology increasingly transforms today's way of life, yet many schools are hardly able to evolve their delivery of content and help students and teachers use these gadgets effectively. On the one hand, students know more than teachers about most technology. On the other, students don't see the value technology offers to further their education.

Can technology really increase learning? If so, how should it be integrated into the curriculum so that it enables students to master subject matter?

Technology and Industry

My students cannot imagine the concept of *cut and paste* in the same way I do, as I was not born in the digital age and because I began working with multimedia production in its analog format. They chuckle at the old way of printing and criticize how much wasteful energy we invested to produce magazines, books, and newspapers. As an industry practitioner, I cannot but appreciate the huge difference in the way the industry functions today. Digital technology revolutionized and streamlined production processes and the frame of mind of those involved.

Students born with new technologies know only about the cut and paste process that doesn't require scissors or glue. They see how it saves time organizing text, photographs, and illustrations for a variety of media applications.

Composing and producing orchestral music for advertisements no longer requires a huge team of musicians and singers. A MIDI player and recorder can simulate the sound of any musical instrument. With a computer system, microphones, and music software, one can record at home with the quality of a studio.

Photography is no longer only an expert's craft as it had been just less than 10 years ago. The publishing industry has dramatically changed its system of accessing high-quality photographs. Publishers lower costs of production by buying digital cameras configured to automatically adjust light and focus. If the art director fails to take a perfect photograph, this can be manipulated with digital imaging software.

Before animation software, it felt like we were shooting cell animation images forever in the studio. We also had to shoot sequentially from the first to the last frames. It was in 1996 when I first worked with a team of animators using 3D animation software and a non-linear editing system. The software created in-between animation sequences, whereas cell animation took hundreds of human in-betweeners to complete a television episode. The software allowed us to work on sequences on a non-linear system and more importantly, to digitally manipulate frames. With the phenomenal software produced by **Softimage** and **Autodesk 3D Studio** we were also able to create and experiment with the combination of 2D and 3D animation.

Many media professions such as animators, photographers, and musicians have been severely impacted by technological changes. Print machine operators needed to study digital printing technologies to keep their jobs. Typists needed to learn encoding with Word. Nurses and doctors needed to attend seminars on new medical software and hardware.

Technology revolutionized all industries, from media to medicine to finance, agriculture to construction to law. Today's industries and professions are shaped by increasing technological innovations in manufacturing, accounting, packaging, distribution, and more.

A cursory check of the classified ads section of daily newspapers reveals how much industries have greater demands for working knowledge of software, for jobs such as architecture and retail that have not traditionally been based on computer systems. For example, not only are accountants expected to have expert knowledge in accounting laws and business finance, today they need to have a working knowledge of business and accounting software as well. A physically demanding position for businesses such as Fedex and the Post Office requires expertise with software. There is hardly any profession today that doesn't function without any computer application.

Students, Teachers, and Digital Technology

By understanding how industries work with digital technologies and by bringing these processes into the design of curricula, teachers will be able to create meaningful learning environments. By merging technology with creative pedagogy and peer-to-peer learning, students will learn from combined real world and classroom experience and be able to create their own theories in similar industry contexts.

It is critical that teachers know how software and hardware function as an integrated system. It is not necessary to master all these technologies. Students who are comfortable with technology should be encouraged to co-teach the class and earn extra credits. While extra credit will be the conscious motivation to teach their classmates in the beginning, eventually these students will realize that by assisting their teachers, they gain confidence, learn more, and are empowered. The teacher learns as well. My best technology teachers were my two teenage sons, who learned software on their own through practice, determination, and by reading manuals.

To illustrate ways of integrating software learning with students in a seamless fashion, this book provides teachers with content-oriented lessons where technology significantly contributes to engaging students in class projects and eventually achieving higher learning results.

The lessons are based on industry practice, where students immerse themselves in projects and activities designed to master the subject

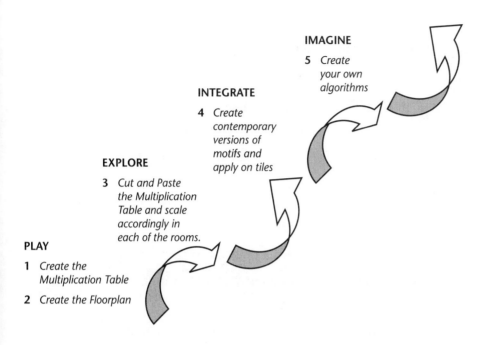

IMAGINE

5 *Create your own algorithms*

INTEGRATE

4 *Create contemporary versions of motifs and apply on tiles*

EXPLORE

3 *Cut and Paste the Multiplication Table and scale accordingly in each of the rooms.*

PLAY

1 *Create the Multiplication Table*

2 *Create the Floorplan*

L
E
A
R
N
I
N
G

H
E
L
I
X

matter. They will learn like they were science, math, language, and social science professionals. The availability of desktop technologies today allows students to create professionally designed multimedia materials, use the Internet for communications and research, and be prepared for the cutting-edge professional demands of industries.

Software Environments

Each program has a graphical user interface (GUI), the visual environment you see on your monitor. For the most part, the programs used in this book provide an intuitive design.

You will find listed below the common elements in these GUIs. Knowing these similar attributes and commands will diminish anxieties about having to learn too much technology. These common elements have the same commands and short cuts as well.

Common Elements

Command	Keyboard Shortcut	Actions
File		
New	Ctrl+N	Creates a new document, new slide, web page, new screen
Open	Ctrl +O	Opens a previously saved file
Close	C	Closes an open file, asking if you wish to save if you have not already saved the document
Save	Ctrl +S	Writes a document to the hard drive
Save As		Saves a copy of a document with another name
Print	Ctrl+P	Opens the printer dialog box and present printing options
Edit		
Undo	Ctrl+Z	Undoes the previous command
Cut	Ctrl+X	Deletes selected text or image
Copy	Ctrl+C	Copies selected text or image
Paste	Ctrl+V	Pastes cut or copied text or image into the current file
Window		Opens a variety of toolboxes. Click on a tool, and a box appears onscreen. To remove toolboxes from screen, click on the X found on right topmost of the box or go back to Window and click to uncheck.
Help		Opens window on questions and answers about the software tools
Ruler		Command to make a ruler visible is found under View

Elements Specific to Programs

Microsoft Word

User works on pages and can edit text, insert text, images, tables, and shapes. Creates documents primarily for print but also offers options for use in web-based applications or slide presentations.

Microsoft PowerPoint

User works on slides and has the option to edit text as well as insert text, images, tables, and shapes. Provides tools to animate presentations. Creates documents primarily for presentations but also offers options for use in web-based or print applications.

Microsoft Excel

User works on spreadsheets to perform calculations. Transforms numbers into charts. Each cell may contain formulas.

Adobe Photoshop and **Photoshop Elements**

User works on canvases to create images and text fonts with options to place images, edit and insert text and tables into the document. It provides tools to design images for the web, print, video, interactive media, and slide presentations.

Ulead VideoStudio and **Apple iMovie**

User works on a Timeline to organize, edit, and combine still and moving text and images to create movies. Both programs provide visual effects, a variety of transitions, and motion effects.

Macromedia Dreamweaver

User works on web pages with tools to create and manipulate images, text, animations and movies for on-line use. The software is designed to enable non-programmers to create web pages with links to other web sites, email addresses, and pages within a web site.

The lesson plans in the next chapters integrate a variety of programs, which are integral to the completion of classroom projects. For example, you will find activities where images in Photoshop will be copied and pasted to other programs. Shapes such as arrows and stars created in Microsoft Office will be copied to other programs where tools are unavailable to create these objects.

VideoStudio works only on a PC, and iMovie works only on a Mac. Otherwise, all the applications used in the book work in both systems.

Both VideoStudio and iMovie accept images, audio, and text produced by any of the rest of the programs, and that could have been created in either one of the operating systems. For example, if you created an image on a PC using Photoshop and saved this as a JPEG, you will be able to copy and paste it on a Mac in iMovie. In much the same way, the VideoStudio will be able to read JPEG images created on a Mac.

The book will engage teachers in a few games, both online and offline. The intent is to experience interactive gaming environments so that teachers can create their own conclusions about gaming and how interactive environments contribute to a 21st century K–12 educational environment.

Peer-to-Peer Learning

In peer-to-peer learning, when students teach they learn more! Managing content delivery through orchestrated peer interactions fosters productive learning experiences. It taps into the unprecedented abilities of the digital generation to learn technology as fast or even faster than their teachers and converts peer pressure to peer support in a cooperative learning culture.

It fosters accountability based on one's unique talents in the context of achieving a collective goal. It is the industry team in action where individual skills, knowledge, and experiences contribute to the success of a project.

When students play the role of teachers and teachers of facilitators, the class becomes a community of learners. It is an inventive, enjoyable, and goal-oriented social learning environment.

I was once tutoring a group of 8- to 10-year-olds once a week in Photoshop, Word, and PowerPoint. The projects they worked on were directly related to their academic classes, defined by a project-based strategy, which included learning software. We worked on science reports, social studies presentations, and English writing publications. As we progressed, the software tools increasingly excited these students. Likewise, they were fascinated by the way their multimedia projects were contributing to raising their grades.

After three two-hour weekly meetings, one or two of them would show me a new technique they discovered with the software. Each week, as soon as they all arrived in the room, an unexpected competition ensued for the best, fastest, and easiest way to achieve an effect on the projects we were working on. They would say, "You can't believe what I just found out," or "I just did something incredibly awesome."

The most amazing aspect of working with these students was that they did not learn tricks from a software manual. They incessantly complained when the hardware system was slow in processing their

P
E
E
R
-
T
O
-
P
E
E
R

L
E
A
R
N
I
N
G

steps. They screamed at the computer when results of their experimentations were different from what they expected. Soon, the overwhelming electricity in the room was powered by their enthusiasm for accomplishing the most fascinating academic-oriented multimedia projects.

On the one hand, while the competition to have the best results kept them going, it also prevented them from appreciating each other's efforts and works. Before long, there was too much showing off among the students, and they would not offer to help each other. I realized that while competition was a driving force in motivating them to learn, among themselves competition was a wedge that blocked the opportunity to share and learn from each other.

Since there were only five students with me in the class, I divided the hours I had each week with them. Every student was to act as the teacher of the group for 15 minutes. During this time, they each had to share with fellow students steps for a specific software effect related to a project we were working on. Each week thereafter, before class started, I reviewed the teaching assignments individually, making sure that they were ready to share their findings to the group. I must say, I learned so much more about software from these kids than I would have done on my own.

I ventured to expand the practice of peer-to-peer learning by giving students extra points if they helped each other in the creation of their projects. The atmosphere in the room changed. Students were no longer only seated down in front of their workstations the whole period. They jumped from seat to seat, demonstrating new-found effects or helping classmates by reviewing previously introduced steps for specific applications.

Structured Learning Activities

Helical Learning lesson plans combine both vertical and horizontal aspects of the learning process. By horizontal, I refer to the Learning Helix, or the process of learning from simple to complex. By vertical,

I refer to the grouping of students in class.

The Learning Helix acts as the spine that guides the teacher in curriculum design. Its four levels provide students with the essential steps in learning about a subject matter. Through these steps, students are provided the fundamentals of content, as well as the mental tools to enable them to comprehend the ramifications of their new-found knowledge. The critical point of learning with this strategy is the learning level called Imagine, when students transform new knowledge about the subject matter to real-world applications.

We will further explore the Learning Helix through a description of a sample mathematics exercise.

Objectives

Students will be able to create their own mathematical algorithms with Excel and Photoshop in the process of designing their own dream homes.

Steps

The activities begin with mathematical fundamentals upon which students will build their algorithms. Reviewing the multiplication table provides the class with a visual framework and builds their confidence, which enables them to understand the process of formulating equations.

Play. The lesson begins with students opening Excel. They create a multiplication table by manually inputting the numbers into each cell.

Explore. The students create a house floor plan using the multiplication table they created, which they copy and paste into Photoshop. The table here plays the dual function of a visual mathematical tool as well as tiling material for a floor plan. As they accomplish these steps, students learn about Excel and Photoshop tools and how they work together to enhance the learning process.

Integrate. The teacher asks students to go to the web and look for a visual motif representing some kind of traditional design from their home or ancestral nation. They bring this into Photoshop and manipulate it to create their own contemporary interpretation of a tile motif using paint and drawing tools. Then they apply the tile design to the floor plan.

Imagine. This is the apex of the learning process. The students compute the total number of tiles with and without visual motifs using the multiplication table as their guide. Students will have to create their own mathematical algorithms with X as the missing answer they will need to solve.

Reflection Questions

The teacher uses questions such as, "How many multiplication tables did you cut and paste onto the floor plan? How many of these tables were complete and how many were parts of a multiplication table? How many tiles are in the incomplete tables?" The teacher moves around each of the groups to clarify confusing concepts and explain rules of mathematical equations. He uses this as an opportunity to review what goes first in an equation, multiplication or addition? Division or subtraction? He may also provide more input on functions in equations.

For this lesson the teacher does not expect students' totals and equations to be completely correct. The lesson is designed for students to have a better appreciation of how equations are created by integrating the standard rules of mathematical operations. As there is no single correct answer for the question, students can brainstorm and free their minds from the fear of not getting the right answer.

Skills and Knowledge Goals

To master the concept of equations, students will have to provide reasons for the ways in which they formulated their equations. The teacher explains, "You will have to explain your formulations the same way mathematicians do in the real world." Particularly for students struggling with mathematical processes, the exercise offers them the opportunity to correlate visual tiles with the multiplication table and then the table with grouping numbers and numerical operations.

The students present their equations to the class with a series of slides using PowerPoint. The software and the need to convince the class of their inventive application of the activity, requires a logical organization of ideas. Moreover, the process passionately engages students as the class discussion revolves around their invented algorithms. They clearly have a stake in the discussion. The teacher asks students to formulate their own conclusions about equations and how these are formulated to solve for X.

Class Structure

Is it better to have class projects accomplished by individuals or by groups? The goal of grouping students is to manage the delivery of content in a way that learners are able to harness their own intelligences and individual resources and apply these to the study of subject matter. Every student should be able to contribute to and grow from the process. The group should benefit from the individual and the individual from the group.

It is also important that students should not be stressed out by assignments they are not ready to fulfill. The classroom environment should be supportive of all types and levels of students. A lack of sensitivity to the abilities of students to work by themselves and with groups will result in lower achievements and chaos in the classroom.

There is a need to employ both individual and group-oriented activities to train students in individual accountability and teamwork; this is the way it works with professional organizations. The guiding principle defines what the teacher wants students to get from the activities and for students to value each one's abilities, contribute, and equally benefit in the learning process.

It helps to combine mixed levels and abilities of students. The project should be encompassing various levels of students in the class. Make sure that in grouping students, activities are designed with both clear individual responsibilities and group goals. Always explain your rubric for grading participation.

Effective Techniques

The learning atmosphere is profoundly influenced by the way a teacher works with her students. After all is said and done, what will make or break our students' desire to learn is our relationship with each one of them. Teaching is not only about lecturing, inputting information, or testing knowledge. In fact, it is an intricate web of interactivity between teacher and students. I liken this to an interactive theater performance. The tone of your voice, your choice of words, the content of your statements, side remarks, the way you stand, sit, dress, and the manner by which you work with your students, all impact the way your students respond to the lesson. The teacher largely defines the learning culture in the classroom.

A teacher may have the most cutting-edge and engaging curriculum, yet if she comes to class with a stern, cold, and unfriendly tone, students will resist or feel uneasy working with her. The emotional climate is a defining factor in keeping students engaged and excited. Some teachers refuse to act like performers in front of the class. Try going to church and listening to a boring pastor or to a political campaign and listening to a lifeless political speaker and you will know how your students feel in a class with a monotonous teacher's voice. Effective facilitation and instruction in a dynamic learning process is like performing in a one-actor interactive theater.

Your energy and enthusiasm will have to compete with the barrage of media students are surrounded by every day. If you have to explain anything, make sure you don't lecture for more than 15 minutes. Connect with your students' interests. Also, while most will be fascinated by your explanation or demonstration, you will need to constantly draw in the one or two minds drifting away. In a friendly tone, ask them a question, call their names, or say a joke about drifting spirits. Don't allow them to get away from learning.

Timing and Rhythm

As in a theatrical performance or a multimedia presentation, every class needs a beginning, middle, and end. You will need to introduce the topic and emotionally gather students' mindsets to the subject matter. Then, as it is in a movie or play, there should be rising action, where you dig deeper into the subject matter and have students increasingly engaged in the activities. The climax is when they discover something new about the subject matter and recognize their newly found abilities in relation to the class project.

A 21st century teacher needs to be a tech-savvy scriptwriter, manager, director, actor, communicator, and friend of his or her students. He has to be as imaginative as he envisions his class, inventive in approaching tasks, and knowledgable about the learning process. Likewise, he has to understand the psychology, intelligences, needs, wants, and abilities of students in the same way an entrepreneur would in business. Teaching is like marketing: you need to know your market and respond to its needs.

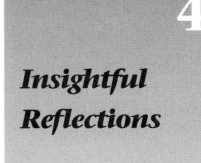

How do students learn theories in science, math, and social science through hands-on projects?

It seems to be the question with the most obvious answer, yet so much depends on the strategies used by the teacher. Every learning activity increases value with theories generated during and after the project. For example, by reviewing the experiences and outcomes of a science project on the impact fast foods have on young people's nutrition, students may learn how to interest their friends, how camera angles affect interviewees, methods of scientific inquiry, and more.

Hands-on projects provide active engagement of students in mastering skills and meaningful experiences that connect learning to real life. More important, these experiences stimulate students to participate in discussions and create their own conclusions.

This chapter describes how to distill theories from practice. It also describes how teachers can effectively guide students to use resources on the web and in libraries to raise standards for learning.

Experience

Learning begins by engaging students in actual projects. It is critical that the teacher provide students with sufficient guidelines to successfully implement their projects. These guidelines include goals, steps, and milestones. Remember, though, guidelines should be looked at as a starting point and not as an end in themselves. Guidelines serve to help students tap into their creativity, from which they spawn new ideas that address critical issues.

By testing their ideas with real projects that evoke responses from others, students come face to face with variables that affect the appropriate use of their creativity, knowledge, and skills.

Education becomes grounded on the importance of learning by working with and contributing to the growth of a civilized world. Learning becomes a community experience. As the student participates in actual projects and makes a difference, he or she takes greater root in the community.

With digital media and the web, the sense of community is expanded from the classroom to the world. Projects in a classroom may be implemented with a school of the same age group of students in another country or state.

Reflect

Projects are subdivided into four general phases in the Helical Learning strategy. These include Play, Explore, Integrate and Imagine. Teachers must engage students in reflective activities in every step of the way. Insightful reflection helps students develop critical thinking and distill lessons in a manner that will increase the opportunities for successes and raise their knowledge about the subject matter.

Begin with the Subjective

Key to healthy classroom discussions is the participation of as many students as possible. Initial questions should ease anxieties about their inabilities to comprehend the subject matter. This can be achieved by asking questions that address the subjective, such as, "What were your highs and lows during the activity? How did you feel about accessing the web for images?"

Mostly, students will respond with answers such as, "I felt good about.... I didn't feel great about.... It was fun!" These answers are stepping stones to higher learning questions. The teacher's goal is to get students involved with non-threatening questions. Effective pedagogy includes the teacher's ability to engage students in active participation about collective and individual experiences in the context of a project and, when possible, to expand the discussion to related experiences beyond the project. By sharing about an experience, students learn a life skill, articulating and communicating key aspects of an experience.

Categorize

In the real world, the success of an endeavor is measured in terms of what worked and what didn't work. In relation to knowledge and skills, this becomes a decisive test of relevance and affectivity.

At this juncture of the reflection process, the teacher contextualizes the meaning of knowledge and skills as a set of abilities that affect results. For example, when students test their alternative recipes for fast food with their peers, the responses of their peers will reflect the success of their experiment.

Did your target community respond positively to your alternative? How do you measure their responses? What did the recipients like and not like? By asking fact-based questions such as these, the teacher uses the experience to introduce students to methods of scientific inquiry—whether this is a project in language arts, math, science, or the social sciences.

Interestingly, while student responses are clearly influenced by collective experiences, their perspectives may reflect differences in judgment over what actually occurred. When this happens, the teacher should ask students to differentiate between fact and judgment. The reflection process offers the teacher an opportune moment to educate the class on the implications of objective and subjective statements in deriving the truth or factual information from the experience.

For a class in social science, this is a powerful occasion to introduce the concepts of prejudice and biases created by culture, family upbringing, or economic status. For a class in science, the teacher may use this as an opening to introduce observation skills. For math, the teacher may ask students to review their equations and determine why there are differences in the students' responses.

It is important for teachers not to respond with "No, you're wrong." Instead they can engage students in more inquiry into the subject matter.

Distill Findings

By drawing students into an initial inquiry and analysis about the subject matter, the teacher establishes a set of variables that affect conclusions about the experience. These variables are categorized in an organized fashion. Using this information, the teachers equip students to respond to more complex and substantive aspects of the subject matter.

The class is now ready to look into the reasons of the findings based on their experiences. Sample questions would be, "Why do you think your target community didn't like your alternative to fast food? Why didn't your camera angle objectively reflect the responses of your interviewees? Why did the formula reflect the variables of the givens in the problem?"

Theorize

Mastery of subject matter is achieved when students are able to determine the theoretical reasons of a project's success or lack of success. Referring to the reasons discussed earlier about the affectivity of a project, the teacher guides students in coming up with formulating theories about the subject matter, based on the project experience. The teacher may ask, "If X was considered a variable, then…. If you spent less on seasonings and more on fresh foods, how would you have…. What, therefore is the conclusion we gather from the findings and reasons behind the findings?"

At this final step of questioning, the teacher's goal is to encourage the class to expand their learning by looking into the writings of master scientists, mathematicians, philosophers, or historians who developed earlier theories related to the subject matter.

By going through a reflective process from a collective experience, students are now ready to read, appreciate, and either contest or build on readings and theories written by the masters. This time anchored in real experiences, they are able to muster their insights to a level of comprehension of the topic with emotional confidence and higher critical thinking skills, which significantly contributes to their abilities in achieving subject matter mastery.

5

Purple Frog

Lesson Objectives

- Engage students in online academic research.

- Inspire them to discover the world wide web.

- Introduce digital tools and creative strategies to develop insightful, creative presentations.

- Navigate the web through effective search strategies.

- Formulate and organize content using innovative visual and literary strategies such as cooperative writing and visual communications, combined with creative interactive tools in Word, Photoshop, Photoshop Elements, and PowerPoint.

- Participate in activities that will expand vocabulary and enhance grammatical and speaking skills.

Icons On The Task Bar

Make sure you set up icons of the software and place these on the dock (for Mac users) and the taskbar (for PC users). In this way, your students will not have to go back to the Directory to open programs.

Format

The lesson progresses from simple to complex activities, culminating in poems, content-oriented imagery, and animated free-verse presentations. Students learn three software tools and web search strategies and integrate them into the final presentation.

Approach

The activities are introduced with a generic topic, which is the Purple Frog. The focus of the chapter will be in the lesson's learning strategy and technology. Specific applications for subject areas are provided in the next chapter.

Tools Needed

- Internet access
- Word, PowerPoint, and Photoshop
- Large screen display

Activity 1, Play: Web Hunting

Objectives

- Check the knowledge of students about the web and search engines.
- Introduce effective and fun search strategies through a web hunting game.
- Build interest in the web as an incredible information resource through challenging but achievable goals.

Instructions

1 Ask students to raise their hand if they have done a web search. Count the number of hands and acknowledge their experiences

by asking, "What can you share with the class about your web search experiences?"

2 After two or three responses, tell the class that you will be asking them to look for some very unusual objects on the web.

3 Instruct them to open a web browser. In the address bar, type and press the Enter key. Instruct them to click the Image tab. Type "yellow forest" and click Google Search.

4 Ask students, "What does Google tell you about the yellow forest?"

5 Begin the race for images. Explain to the students that they are going to race each other and that this going to be a fun game. You will say, "Find a pink diamond. Start!" When a student finds the object, check the monitor, and if you see a pink diamond, ask the student to come forward and type in the web site address and explain how they found the object. Encourage the rest of the class to check to see whether the site has a pink diamond.

6 Write the letter *Y* on the board and say, "Look for inverted *Y*s." When a student finds the object ask him or her to come forward and type in the address they went to and to explain how they found the object. Encourage the rest of the class to see if the web site does have an inverted *Y*.

Need	Strategy
You are looking for specific phrases, e.g., "jumping purple frog."	Type the "word" or "phrase" in quotation marks.
You are looking for general definitions about a topic, e.g., purple frog.	Type words referring to the topic, reformulate until you get results
You are looking for IMAGES, e.g., pink diamonds.	Type words in quotation marks, e.g., "pink diamonds" and choose IMAGE or PICTURE button.

Write down key word responses from students on the board in an organized format. This will help in structuring their thoughts.

7   Instruct them to go to www.yahoo.com. Say, "Find a pair of orange eyes for me." Write the words "orange eyes" on the board. When a student finds the object, ask him or her to come forward and type in the address they went to and to explain how they found the object. Encourage the rest of the class to check.

8   Instruct them to go to www.alltheweb.com. and tell them to look for five purple frogs.

9   Tell students to type their full names in any of the search engines. Discuss any information that has to do with their names.

Keyword Responses

To assist students in formulating conclusions about an activity or topic, you choose a word/words that embrace essential ideas of the lesson. Specifically for the web search activity, the following terms are useful: Find, My Name, Images, Variety of Media, Movies, Keywords, and Quotation Marks.

Reflection

Review the activity with the class. Ask students questions that will engage their critical and evaluative thinking skills. Some of these questions may include:

1   What did you discover about the web?

Sample Answers

- I didn't know that I could find my name on the web. It's shocking!

- You can also find images using search engines.

- Most search engines help you find text and provide searches for a variety of media like still images and movies.

2   How can you use search engines to find information?

Sample Answers

- Search engines have similar and also special tools.

- If you want answers to questions, use www.askjeeves.com. If you want a specific topic, use www.google.com.

- Searching the web is all about using the right word. Sometimes the responses are not what you're looking for, so you need to reformulate your keywords or use quotation marks.

- Advertisers control some search engines. You don't really get the results you need.

Write down key word responses from the students on the board and summarize.

Summary

Tips for searching the web: it's all about using the right keywords or phrases.

1 If you know exactly what you're looking for, use specific keywords related to the topic. If you don't know exactly what you're looking for, begin with a phrase or so, and then use the results to help you define what you're looking for.

You are looking for specific phrases, for example, *jumping purple frog.* Type the phrase in quotation marks. You are looking for general definitions about a topic, for example, *purple frog.* Type words referring to the topic. If you want an overview definition, type the words *purple frog.*
If unsatisfied with the results reformulate your keywords. You are looking for images, for example, *pink diamonds.* Type the words in quotation marks.

2 The web provides information in a variety of media.

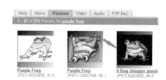

Activity 2, Explore: Top Ten Search Engines

Objectives

Learn about the top 10 search engines by engaging students in a race. Identify various types of search engines and learn to cite web sources of their information through a fun research activity.

Instructions

1 Arrange students into three groups. Tell them they will be using the *web search strategies* discussed in the reflection. Briefly review these strategies with your class. Each of the groups will look for a list of the top 10 search engines on the web. They will need to cite their source and the date the list was made.

2 Provide each of the groups a big 3x3-foot sheet with three columns. Column one is the top 10 search engines, and column two contains reasons why they are in the top 10. The first team that finishes passes their sheet to you, and they receive five points for being first. The second team gets three points, and the third team one point.

3 Post the sheets on the board. Review the lists and pinpoint the most popular 10 search engines by counting each of the items. Ask students to help you with the counting. Tally the score.

Reflections

It is crucial to provide students the opportunity to participate in identifying key points of an exercise. The following are suggested questions that may engage their critical thinking on the research findings:

1 What did you find out about search engines in the activity we just accomplished?

Sample Answers:

- There are so many types of search engines.

Using Search Engines

Experienced Web users usually already have their own favorite search engines. Mostly, this is based on familiarity with the interface and popularity among peers. However, it is useful to know what makes a constantly innovating technology powerful and relevant for teachers and students.

Top 10 Search Engines	
1. google.com	largest index results
	adds phrases to its dictionary to improve relevance of results
2. cantreadit.com	clear, organized information
SOURCE :www.noodletools.com DATE LIST WAS MADE.12/03/03	

- I didn't know Yahoo was a search engine.

- What's the difference between a search engine and a library, for example, or the "Librarian's Index to the Internet"?

2 How can these search engines help students and professionals succeed?

Sample Answers:

- If you know which search engine can best find your information, you will accomplish your research right away.

- Search engines are like taxi drivers—they drive you to the place you're looking for.

Summary

- Search engines facilitate research on almost anything and everything.

- Search engines are electronic and globally linked information catalogs that facilitate navigation in the web.

- Search engines provide students with the technology to access information. It is the equivalent of a global data library at your fingertips. You can also find information of various formats on the web.

- Search engines have their public and commercial versions. Usually, the public version is limited while the commercial version, which requires a monthly or annual fee to use provides a more extensive source of information. In most cases for the K–12 education community, the public versions of search engines are more than enough to access relevant and timely information and images.

Activity 3, Integrate: Search Strategies and Purple Frog

Objectives

Students will be able to create their own conclusions about the best search strategies and search engines through a hands-on activity such as the *Purple Frog*. They will integrate tools in three programs: Photoshop, PowerPoint, and Word. The class will merge multiple-intelligence abilities with creative insight by producing a meaningful literary and animated presentation on Purple Frog.

Instructions

1 Point to the web addresses discovered by the winning participants of the five purple frog race. Tell the class to type any of these addresses in a search engine of their choice. Their task is to choose one purple frog.

2 Underscore the need for the frog to be purple. Instruct students to right-click on the purple frog of their choice. A menu will pop up. Tell them to select Copy and then minimize the browser by clicking on the minus sign in the upper-right corner of the window.

3 On the task bar, click the Word icon.

4 Click on File and then New. A dialog screen will appear. Choose Blank and then click OK.

5 Inform students that this is a creative writing exercise. They will use Word because it provides them with writing tools such as Edit, Cut, Spelling, Grammar, and the Thesaurus. As you explain, show the location of these tools on the screen. Type in a word sample and expound on the functionalities of these tools and their importance in writing.

You may say, "In writing we don't always have the most appropriate word for what we want to say. If we were writing on a

piece of paper and using a pencil, we are constantly worried about immediately having the right word to avoid erasures on our paper."

Word recognizes these challenges and provides users with options to present a professional-looking paper. When you Edit and Cut, you erase without leaving any mark. When you are in search of synonyms or the most appropriate word to use in a sentence or phrase, you can click Tools, choose Language and Thesaurus. There you will find a list of synonyms and options for more synonyms if you select a word. Then click Look Up.

6 Begin the activity. First, go to Edit and then Paste. The purple frog you chose from the web should appear on your documents. On the toolbar, click on Center Margin. The image of your purple frog should now be at the top center of your document. Press Enter twice to create two spaces below the image.

Active Participation

By getting students physically up and about in a beginning activity, the teacher eases their anxieties about writing and builds their confidence for more complex projects later in the lesson.

7 Look at your frog and then write a phrase that describes its most striking features. You can choose to tell about its color, texture, action, lines, dots, shapes, etc.

> *Eg. Slimy, shiny purple skinned frog*

8 Ask students to move one seat to their right. Read the phrase the author wrote about the frog that is now in front of you. You will add more phrases to the one already written. Specifically, in one to three phrases, using your imagination, describe the place or setting where you see the frog. The place should be different from the taken from the web.

> *Eg. You're sitting on my coffee table and watching me*
> *Drink my morning liquid perk up formula.*

9 Each time students are done with the task, ask the class to move one seat to the right. They will read the phrase the author wrote about the frog in the next workstation and add more phrases to the one already written. Following are the contents of the phrases they will need to write as they move to a new workstation:

Third move: Describe the eyes of the frog. Then add a commentary on what you think or feel about these eyes. If the image has no visible eyes, create one using your imagination.

> *Eg. Uneven, unpredictable.*
> *Why are your eyes so droopy?*

> *Eg. You are an assortment of purple patches.*

Fourth move: Imagine what's in the mind of the frog at that moment.

> *Eg. The Aspens, they are turning yellow at this time of year.*

> *Eg. You say you want to go home. But where is home for you?*
> *You miss your friends and family. Are they not in the city*
> *where you live?*

Fifth move: Imagine and describe how the frog feels at that moment.

Eg. You say you feel alone, like you have no friend in the world.

Sixth move: Imagine and describe what you want to do for or with the frog.

> *Eg. All right, jump on my palm and I'll take you where your spirit is craving to be.*

10 Finally, ask the students to go back to their original seats and then read all the phrases added to their first lines about the frog. Instruct them to imagine and write one or two phrases about what the frog is telling them about life.

> *Eg. After all, you strive to be one with the craziness of this world.*

11 Tell them to review the lines as if these were part of a poem—connect the logic of each of the parts without reorganizing the order of the lines.

> Edit the poem. If you find words underlined in red, this means Word is detecting a spelling error. Click Tools on the toolbar and choose Spelling & Grammar. If words are underlined in green, this means Word is detecting a grammatical error. Click Tools and choose Spelling & Grammar.

12 Instruct students to print one copy of their poems.

13 Students love to write poems and read them to their friends. You may encounter some resistance to reading aloud in this part of the activity, but it will be minimal. Say, "You will read aloud your poems to the class. We will begin from left moving clockwise to the right."

Instant Gratification

Gen-Y students are growing up with new media, which are interactive interfaces that provide instant gratification. The use of MS Word in a creative writing exercise helps them to immediately recognize and fix their spelling and grammar mistakes.

Printers & Printing

To print, go to File and choose Print. The Print Dialog Box appears.

For Laser printers, check the paper tray and make sure sheets are available. Then click OK.

For deskjet and Inkjet printers, check the paper tray and make sure sheets are available. To minimize ink usage, click on Properties, choose Draft and click OK. Click OK again in the Print Dialog Box.

Activity 4, Imagine, Part 1: Visualizing Poetry and Purple Frog

Objectives

Tackle The Learning Curve

Initially, learning Adobe Photoshop/Elements may seem tedious and confusing. That's because there are so many tools, and the procedures tend to be complex at the start. The lesson plans in this book provide for timely reviews of these procedures.

- Students will interpret their poems with visual images taken from the web by copying, pasting, and manipulating these images with Photoshop.

- They will acknowledge web sources of their images as an element of sound academic research.

- Finally, they will create and manipulate images to visually communicate thoughts and emotions to audiences by using and integrating graphics tools such as Photoshop and PowerPoint.

Image Proportions

By holding down the Shift key while transforming, the user maintains the proportion of the manipulated image.

Instructions

Purple Frogs 1 and 2

1 Instruct students to click on the purple frog image in the Word document. When they see a black frame around the document, they should go to Edit and choose Copy.

2 Click on the Photoshop icon on the dock (for Mac users) or the taskbar (for PC users).

3 Check the Auto Select Layer box in the upper left corner of the window. Layers can be tricky for new users of Adobe Photoshop/Elements. Doing this allows users to click on an image and the Layer tool will automatically shift to that image's layer.

4 Click File on the toolbar, and choose New. A File dialog box will appear. Fill in the blanks and click OK. I recommend the following setup.

Name	*Purple Frog*
Width	6 inches
Height	6 inches
Resolution	72 dpi
Mode	RGB

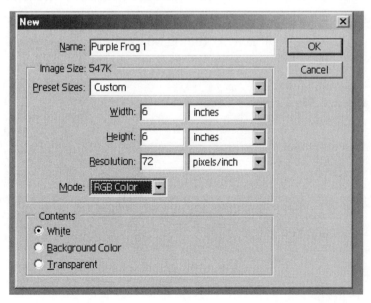

Toolbar

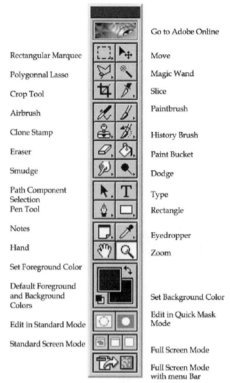

New Window

File Size = Resolution

When bringing in a graphics image from the Web and other sources, Photoshop/Elements automatically reads the File Size. You will see this in the New Dialog box.

Minimize A File

To minimize a file means to keep the document open and available in the task bar. This allows the user to multitask (to simultaneously work on several documents and programs).

---

5 Briefly introduce Photoshop and Photoshop Elements. Both are graphics programs used primarily to manipulate pictures and create visual images. Both have similar tools. Photoshop is the industry standard. Elements is a pared down version that is fine for simple digital image manipulation techniques.

6 In Word, instruct students to go to Edit, Copy. They should then open the Photoshop software and click on New. The New Dialog box appears. Tell the class to type the filename as: Purple Frog 1; file size, 8" x 8"; color as, RGB; and to maintain the default white background.

   After filling the dialog box, press Enter. A New Document appears. The same purple frog in their Word document should be in their graphics document. To do this, they should go to Edit and click Paste. The purple frog should appear on the digital canvas.

7 Inform students that they will be duplicating Purple Frog 1. Click Image and choose Duplicate. A Duplicate Image dialog box will appear. Complete as: Purple Frog 2; file size, 8" x 8"; color, RGB and to maintain the default white background. Click OK.

8 To safeguard each of the files, instruct your students to separately save them as PSD file extensions. To do this, click on File, choose Save As. A Save As dialog box appears. Choose a direc-

---

Graphics File Format Extensions

.psd native Photoshop file, with independent layer system, mostly used for manipulating images

.gif compressed file format mostly used with flat-colored images on the Web

.jpeg compressed file format mostly used for Web-based images, contains more complex color spectrums and patterns and is also used in still pictures for video and MS powerpoint.

tory to save the files and then create a new folder by clicking the "Create a new directory" button. Give the directory a name such as "Purple Frog," and then name the file appropriately and click OK. Repeat this routine for all four files.

9   Minimize all the files except for Purple Frog 1.

10 To clean up the original background of the purple frog, use the magic wand tool. Click on the background of the image. Students will be able to recognize if they are doing the command correctly if "running ants," or a selection marquee, move along the sides of the image.

lasso tool

11 Another way to select the background for deletion is to use any of the Select tools. The easiest one to manipulate is the Polygonal Lasso tool. Students will click on the tool, then click on a part of the edge of the image they want to select, drag the mouse to a few pixels and then click and stretch again and so on until they surround the circles with dots and lines with the Polygonal Lasso tool. To close the circle, double-click the Cursor tool.

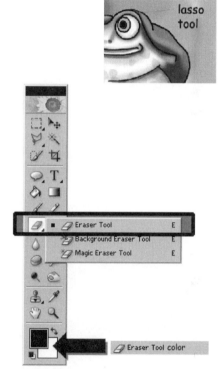

12 As with the magic wand, students will be able to recognize if they are doing this command correctly if a selection marquee, likened to running ants, moves along the sides of the image.

13 Press the Delete key or use the Eraser tool to remove the background. Adjust the eraser size to fit the area for erasing by clicking the inverted triangle of the brush tool on the toolbar. A drop-down menu will provide them with options. Students can choose whatever size of eraser will work for their background clean up. Click the area to remove from the background and drag the mouse, as if painting with a brush.

Eraser Tool color

14 For the areas close to lines, it is advisable to magnify the image by going to the toolbox and clicking on the Zoom tool (which looks like a magnifying glass) and clicking on the area they are working on. If students work on bigger pixels as they erase, they are most likely to come up with cleaner and more accurately

Eraser

The Eraser tool takes its color from the lower blank square image in the lower part of the toolbox.

Layers

Layers are your best friends in Photoshop/Elements. In the beginning, as you climb the learning curve, they tend to be confusing. By selecting the Auto Select Layer tool, users will simply have to click on the image's part and the layer will change accordingly.

Layers and Maneuverability

With the layering tool, Photoshop allows you to create more than 1,000 independent layers in a single file, depending on hard drive memory. By layering images, you will be able to manipulate them more efficiently, without affecting other parts of the object.

Hierarchy Of Layers

Layers are arranged in a vertical hierarchical order in the Layer box. The higher the layer the more forward they are in position.

If you don't see your Layer Box on the screen, click on Window and check Show Layers.

It is useful to have the Layer Box opened as you carry on your procedure.

Frustrated With Layers?

Give it a chance. With constant use, you will get used to their nature. In the long run, layers provide maneuverability and flexibility in manipulating images.

Layers and Transparencies

I liken layers to transparencies. You can't physically see them. They are also arranged one on top of the other.

With layers, one can edit and manipulate an image without affecting the other parts.

Flattened And Layered Images

The image files will be brought into MS powerpoint in the latter part of the lesson. In this context, some image files need to be flattened. Flattened images will be saved in JPEG extension format.

To provide students with the option to revise their files, as they complete the lesson, they will save a separate unflattened image file in PSD extension format.

flattened images equals a single layer

manipulated images. Explain to them that they will create a background for the purple frog that is different from the current background. The new background should be based on the second line of the poem.

15 To capture the background image, instruct them to go to a search engine of their choice and choose Photos or Images in the Edit bar. They will type key words referring to the background image.

16 As soon as they find the background material, they will right-click on the image and a drop-down menu appears. Choose Copy.

17 Go to Photoshop, choose File, New. A New dialog box appears. They type the title, Background, and click OK.

18 To merge the background with the purple frog, students will click firmly, hold, and drag the background from its canvas to the Purple Frog 2 canvas.

19 To position the background image behind the purple frog, students should go to the Layer box and drag and drop the layer of the background image below the image of the purple frog.

click, drag & drop the photograph to the frame of the purple frog

20 Adjust the purple frog to fit the background. Since these two images were taken from separate sources, they probably don't match in terms of size and perspective. To resize, click Edit and choose Free Transform. Hold the Shift key down while resizing and drag the square pegs at the corner of the images. To turn the image left, right, or around, click Edit and choose Transform. A menu appears. Choose from any of the five options—scale, rotate, skew, distort, and perspective, for the desired results.

18 Guide the students to merge the purple frog with the background image with the shadow tool. Go to Layer, choose Layer Style and then Drop Shadow. A Layer Style dialog box appears. Experiment and check tools on the left column. Experiment

with this visual effect by manipulating the drop shadow structure and quality. Click OK when done.

19   Duplicate the image and keep one original layered copy. A dialog box appears. Click on Image, choose Duplicate, and then give the copy a filename, Purple Frog 2 copy, and click OK.

20   Flatten the image copy. Go to Layer and choose Flatten Image.

21   Save the three images, one at a time. Go to File and choose Save As. Go to the appropriate directory, choose the Purple Frog folder, choose PSD as file extension for the layered image and JPEG for the flattened image, and click Save. Finally, save Purple Frog 1, now without a background with the JPEG extension file in the same folder.

Purple Frog 3

22   Minimize all Purple Frog images except for Purple Frog 2.psd. Go to Image and Duplicate Image. Save the new file as Purple Frog 3.psd.

23   This time students will enlarge the eyes of the frog. Click on the Zoom Tool and bring the magnifying glass icon on top of one of the eyes of the frog. Click to enlarge the image.

24   Select the eye by clicking the Polygonal Lasso tool, and then surround the eye of the purple frog with the Lasso tool.

25   To enlarge the eyes, click Edit, choose Free Transform, hold down the Shift key and stretch any of the square pegs. When the eye is big enough, press Enter. Do the same with the other eye.

26   When done, duplicate the image and keep one original layered copy.
     A dialog box appears. Click on Image, choose Duplicate, and then give the copy a filename, Purple Frog 3 copy, and click OK.

27   Flatten the image copy. Go to Layer and choose Flatten Image.

28 Save the flattened and unflattened files with the same names in the Purple Frog folder. Keep the unflattened file open and close the flattened file.

Purple Frog 4

29 Create an image that visualizes thoughts in the frog's mind.

30 Duplicate the unflattened file of Purple Frog 3 and name it Purple Frog 4. Close the Purple Frog 3 image.

31 Following the same steps as in Purple Frog 3, direct students to go to the web and find images that appropriately describe what is in the frog's mind at that moment. Capture these images to Photoshop as new files. Name each of the files and click OK.

32 Students will click, drag, and drop the image that represents what is in the frog's mind at that moment to the Purple Frog 4 file. To ensure the image is above all other layers on this file, they must go to the Layers palette and drag the file of this

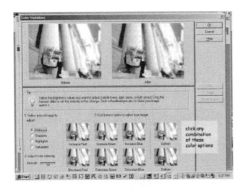

image to the highest vertical position.

33 To visually connect the image to the frog's mind, instruct students click the Brush tool. The toolbars will change accordingly to brush options.

Tell them to choose the solid brush, size 25, and opacity 100 percent. Then they can choose a color at the lower end of the toolbar. Click on the Set Foreground Color box, and the Color Picker dialog box appears. Students click on a color and click OK.

34 Using the Brush tool, students will draw a callout around the mental image visually linked to the mind of the frog.

35 They duplicate the image and keep one original layered copy. A dialog box appears. Click on Image, choose Duplicate, give the copy a filename, purple frog 4 copy, and click OK.

36 Flatten the image copy. Go to Layer and choose Flatten Image.

37 Save the flattened and unflattened files with the same names in the Purple Frog folder. Keep the unflattened file open and close the flattened file.

Purple Frog 5

38 Students will transform the color of the frog to visually portray its feelings at that moment.

39 Duplicate the unflattened file of Purple Frog 4 and name it Purple Frog 5. Close Purple Frog 4.

40 To remove the callout and the mental image of the frog, tell students to go to the Layers palette and click on the layers of the

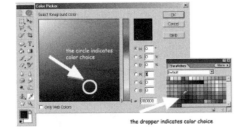

Choosing Color

If the students correctly followed the steps to choose color from the Color Picker, they will see their chosen palette color in the Set Foreground Color.

callout and the mental image, then click and drag these one by one to the trash located at the lower right of the Layers palette.

41 Engage students in a discussion about color and its correlation to feelings. For example, when you say "I feel blue…" or when one feels "red…" What emotions do each of the colors associates with?" Conclude the discussion by summarizing color as a visual symbol of an emotion. Proceed with the activity by instructing students to describe the frog's feelings at this moment by changing its color tones.

42 Tell students to go to Image, Adjust, and Variations. The Variations dialog box will appear. Consider these tools like they were paint colors that you add or subtract in an image. Additionally, on the right side of the dialog box, there are options for adjusting lightness and darkness. Use the Current Pick version as the color status of the image as you manipulate with these tools. Students can experiment by clicking the various tones on the dialog box to create the color that describes the frog's feelings at that moment.

43 Duplicate the image and keep one original layered copy. A dialog box appears. Click Image, choose Duplicate and name the file purple frog 5 copy.

44 Flatten the image copy. Go to Layer, and choose Flatten Image.

45 Save flattened and unflattened files with the same names in the Purple Frog folder. Keep the unflattened file open and close the flattened file.

Purple Frog 6

46 Explain to the students that they will each bring an image from the web that describes what they want to do with the frog in Photoshop.

47 Duplicate the unflattened file of Purple Frog 5 and name it Purple Frog 6. Close the Purple Frog 5 image.

48 Students will paste the image from the web to the topmost layer of Purple Frog 6

49 This is a review step. Tell students they can adjust the background and the frog images as they wish.

50 Duplicate the image and keep one original layered copy. A dialog box appears. Click on Image, choose Duplicate and then name file Purple Frog 6 copy.

51 Flatten the image copy. Go to Layer and choose Flatten Image.

Purple Frog 7

52 Explain to the students that they will each capture an image that describes the poem's insight about life from the web to Photoshop.

53 Duplicate the unflattened file of Purple Frog 6 and name it Purple Frog 7. Close the Purple Frog 6 image.

54 Students will drag and drop the way the frog poetry reflects about life image into the Purple Frog 7 file.

55 This is a review step. Tell students they can adjust the back-

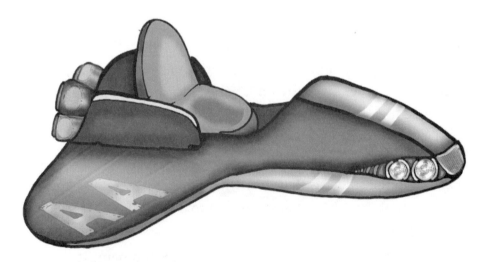

ground and the frog images as they wish.

56 Duplicate the image and keep one original layered copy. A dialog
box appears. Click on Image, choose Duplicate and name the file
Purple Frog 7 copy.

57 Assist students in reviewing their files in each of their folders.
Each student should have a total of 14 files: seven files titled
Purple Frog 1-7 with the PSD extension and seven files titled
Purple Frog Copy 1-7 with the JPEG extension.

Reflections

Congratulate the students for their excellent work using sophisticated
graphic software. Remind them that by mastering this software, they
will have added another skill component into their resume, which
will help in future job applications.

Divide the class into groups of five or six students. Instruct them
to answer the following questions and to write their answers on a big
sheet of paper. Remind them that it's important for everyone to contribute. Every high, low, and reflection contributed by the individuals will be valuable lessons for the entire class. They will divide the
paper into three columns and fill the blanks accordingly.

	Lows	Highs	Lessons
Software			
Content			
Process			

Divide the manila paper so that the above elements can guide students in reflecting on the activity.

Summary

- The web provides a gamut of images for students to use as stimuli and material to mold their messages.

- Students need to acknowledge the use of other people's images by citing the web source and author (if possible).

- Photoshop provides a variety of tools to manipulate and shape images according to the message.

- The use of these tools requires an understanding of their capabilities and the step-by-step process to get desired visual results.

Activity 4, Imagine, Part 2: Animating Poetry and Purple Frog

Objectives

Students will organize and animate their visual poetry presentation by integrating text and images in PowerPoint. They will learn how to apply timing and highlight key messages in their presentations by using the animation tools.

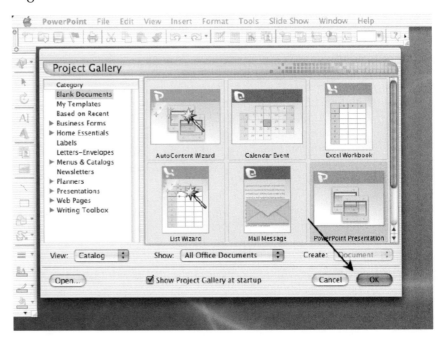

Instructions

1 Open PowerPoint.

2 Check the blank presentation and click OK. Choose the blank square.

3 Briefly describe PowerPoint. Use the introduction in Chapter 1 of the book to guide your explanation. Involve students by asking them to share what they see on their screens.

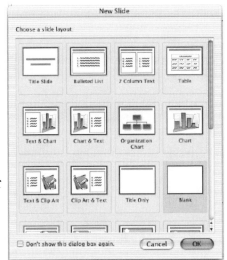

4 Tell students that they will need seven slides for the presentation. To set these up, they will click Insert and Duplicate Slide seven times. The number of slides is visible on the left column of the window in Slide Sorter View.

5 Each of the slides correlates with lines 1 to 7 of the poem and images 1 to 7 from Photoshop. Instruct students to type the lines of the poem matching line 1 with slide 1 and so on. On each of the slides, tell them to click on the icon of the text box found in the Drawing toolbar. When they see the icon dip in the bar, they should click again on the slide. A box with six square pegs appears with a cursor at the center. Type the lines of the poem. The default size of the font in PowerPoint is 24 pt. This is too big for the screens of the poem project. Tell students to highlight the lines and change the size and type as they wish. These tools are found in the top toolbar.

6 There are a variety of ways to integrate images from Photoshop to PowerPoint. For this lesson, I will present one procedure.
   a) Click on the square at the topmost right of the Window. Go to the rightmost edge of the PowerPoint window until your cursor shifts from one arrow to two arrows. Drag the edge to the middle of the screen.

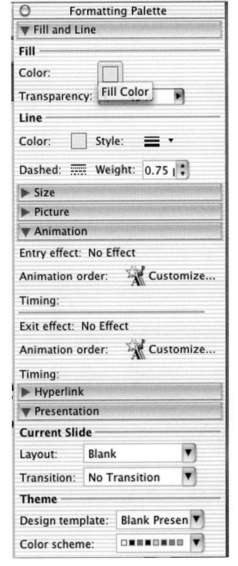

b) Open Photoshop and do a similar procedure, this time using

the Move Tool. Click the leftmost edge and drag this to the middle of the screen.

c) You should have both windows on your screen.

d) Click the Photoshop window and go to File>Open and choose the Purple Frog folder. Double-click on Purple Frog 1.jpg. Click, drag, and drop the image all the way to the PowerPoint window on Slide 1. The image should now be both in Photoshop and PowerPoint. Do the same until all the images are integrated into the PowerPoint.

e) Extend the rightmost edge of the PowerPoint window to the edge of the screen. Check your files. In each of the screens you must have lines of poetry and the image with which the lines correlate.

f) Adjust the text with the image on each of the screens by clicking on the text or image and manipulating the size using the square pegs in the frames.

You are an assortment of purple patches

g) After accomplishing your steps in each of the slides, make sure you go to File and Save File as Purple Frog Animation in the Purple Frog folder.

7 Remind students to close Photoshop when done to avoid memory overload on the computer.

8 Animate the slides, text, and images. Since this is an introductory lesson to the software, the following steps are based on preset animation schemes. Instruct the students to follow these steps:

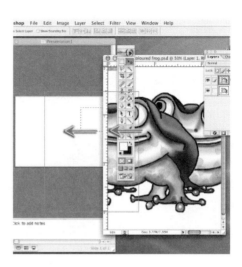

a) You will choose an animation effect for all the text. Highlight the text and click on Slideshow. Choose Custom Animation, and a menu appears. Choose any one of the options.

For purposes of continuity and unity in design, choose only one type of animation effect for the entry of all the text and apply this for the seven slides.

b) You will animate each of the images. Click an image and click on Slideshow. Choose Custom Animation and choose any one of the options.

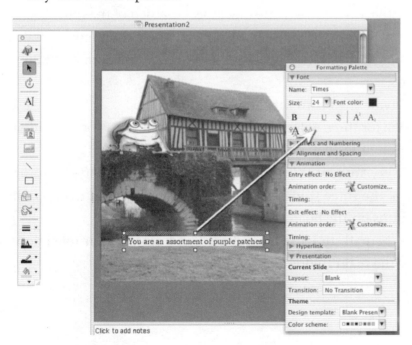

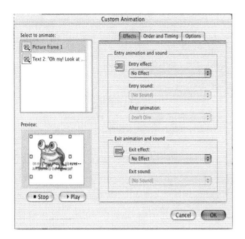

For purposes of continuity and design unity, choose only one type of animation effect for entry of all the images in the seven slides.

c) Review your presentation. Click the first slide on the Slide Sorter, then the Slideshow icon located at the drawing task bar. Click the arrow key to the right to keep the presentation moving.

d) If you need to revise some slides, click on the icon of Normal View beside the Slideshow icon. Proceed with your revisions.

9 Students showcase their work in class. Acknowledge the insights and creative techniques used after each presentation. Then ask students how the creative techniques helped in making the presentation more compelling for the audience.

Reflections

Distribute four pieces of 3.5 x 11-inch plain paper to each student. Instruct them to write the two most difficult and two best aspects of the activity. They will write one aspect on each of the four sheets. Students will write in bold letters, so that their comments can be read from at least 10 feet away. Also, they should use no more than seven words.

Divide the board into three columns.

Ask for three volunteers to stand in front of the board and organize each of the columns according to similar insights.

Every student then reads each of their sheets. After reading, ask any of the three student volunteers to post them in the appropriate columns on the board.

When all students have shared and posted their reflections, review the main trends and significant points.

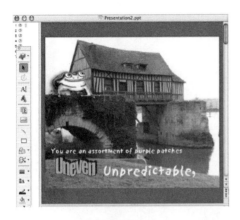

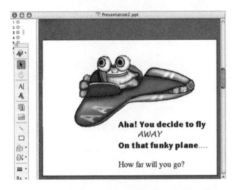

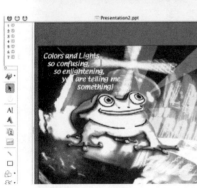

	Lows	Highs	Lessons
Software			
Content			
Process			

Divide the manila paper so that the above elements can guide students in reflecting on the activity.

Summary

- PowerPoint is a multimedia presentation software and has the ability to integrate a variety of file formats. In the case of moving images from Photoshop one can simply open both programs, and then drag and drop from one to the other.

- The creator of the presentation defines the content, flow and pace of the presentation. With effective use of animation tools, presentations come alive and are more compelling.

- When all text and images are prepared beforehand, PowerPoint makes it easy to organize a presentation.

- With digital tools, one can always go back and revise and not worry about the cost of materials.

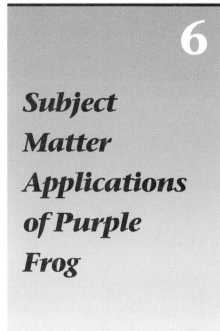

Subject Matter Applications of Purple Frog

Objective

Purple Frog provides an experiential, integrated, and progressive set of activities that engage students in meaningful study of specific subject matter using four digital media software applications: PowerPoint, Photoshop, the Web, and Word. The lesson is designed to meet K–12 education standards in critical thinking, research, writing, communications, and technology.

Additionally, the lesson is geared toward connecting classroom learning with the real world. The culminating project, which is a presentation of the subject matter or topic defined by the teacher and produced by the students, is showcased to a target community audience.

Skills Learned

Students will engage in hands-on web-based research by using effective search strategies and citing sources. The lesson provides students with academic research fundamentals. This is accomplished in a systematic and active manner via a series of activities that progress from simple to complex.

In addition, students will:

- Obtain, organize, and present information, develop and discuss opinions, construct new knowledge, and work cooperatively in teams.

- Explore the concept of the common good and social commitment as they learn more about the topic and learn to listen and respond to their classmates.

- Develop a final project directed towards making a difference in their communities.

- Develop creative, professional-level technology skills.

Format

As an introductory activity to web research, Purple Frog uses images instead of text. In this way, visually oriented students are not overwhelmed by having to read text in addition to following text clues. Also, by using images, the activity broadens the concept of the web as a multimedia information resource.

Approach

The lesson provides students with a step-by-step process for creating a multimedia presentation. Using very powerful and professional-level graphics software, Photoshop, students will be able to manipulate digital images to accurately communicate the message of their presentations.

Following are some examples of courseware applications to K–12 subject areas. The grade level applications are determined by the topic and depth of subject matter mastery.

Science

Play: Web Hunting

Objectives

Introduce a science topic, for example, water and the future of human civilization, and the concept of scientific inquiry by engaging students in finding:

- Images
- Web sites
- Studies
- Scientists involved with the study

Stimulate students' interests in the topic with the use of a fun and effective Web hunting activity.

Explore: Top 10 Search Engines

Objectives

- Increase students' interest in the topic by engaging them in a web search race in the form of images, web sites, studies, or scientists on the topic.
- List reasons why the class needs to learn the topic by citing student research findings in a class discussion.
- Formulate questions and hypotheses about the topic by sifting through the information gathered from the web search activity.

Integrate: Creative Writing Exercise

Expand knowledge and comprehension about the various aspects of the topic by sourcing information from the web in a structure provided by the teacher.

In each of the following steps, write phrases, sentences or paragraphs that respond to these sample questions. The length of information is dependent on the grade level.

Step 1	Why is the topic relevant to students? Cite how the topic affects people today.
Step 2	What are the most important facets of the topic?
Step 3	Who are the people and what variables control the topic?

Broaden and deepen scientific knowledge on the topic through a cooperative writing exercise likened to the poetry writing activity in Purple Frog based on the above questions.

Imagine: Creative Imaging Exercise

Expand perceptions of the subject matter by taking visual images from web sources and manipulating them with Photoshop to fit student explanations about the topic.

Apply sound academic research practice by acknowledging web sources of the images and information they use in their presentations.

Effectively communicate personal and learner insights through visual imagery by using digital graphics tools and oral presentations skills.

Social Science

Play: Web Hunting

Introduce a social science topic for example, the significance of 9/11 for the American people, and find out the various ways the topic is defined by people through images, web sites, studies, and scientists.

Stimulate students' interests in the topic with the use of a fun and effective web hunting activity.

Explore: Differing Perspectives

Increase students' interest in the topic by searching for differing perspectives on it via a web search race in the form of images, web sites, studies, or scientists.

List various perceptions about the topic by citing research findings of the students in a class discussion.

Students will express their own insights through the information gathered from the web search activity.

Integrate: Creative Writing Exercise

Students will expand their knowledge and comprehension about the various aspects of the topic by sourcing information from the web in a content structure provided by the teacher. A sample structure may look like the following:

In each of the following steps, write phrases, sentences or paragraphs that respond to these sample questions. The length of information is dependent on the grade level.

Step 1 Why is the topic relevant to students? How will the topic relate to people's lives in contemporary society?

Step 2 What are the most important facets of the topic?

Step 3 What contexts and other variables affect the decisions related to the topic?

Step 4 What insights about the topic do students derive from their findings?

Students will broaden and deepen their knowledge on the topic through a cooperative writing exercise based on the above questions.

Imagine: Creative Imaging Exercise

Expand perception of the subject matter by taking visual images from web sources and manipulating them using Photoshop to fit student explanations.

Apply sound academic research practice by acknowledging web sources of the images and information they use in their presentations.

Effectively communicate personal and learner insights through visual imagery with digital graphics tools and multimedia presentations skills.

Math

Play: Web Hunting

Introduce a mathematic concept in its abstract and concrete form, for example, statistics and probability, by sourcing information from the web in the form of images, or web sites.

Stimulate students' interests in the topic with the use of a fun and effective web hunting activity.

Explore: Topic Applications

Increase students' interest in the topic by searching about applications of the mathematical concepts about the topic.

List various applications of the topic by citing research findings of the students in a class discussion.

Students create their own formulations and applications about the topic with information gathered from the web search activity.

Integrate: Creative Writing Exercise/Math Writing

Expand students' knowledge and comprehension about the mathematical concept by sourcing information from the web in a structure provided by the teacher. A sample structure may look like the following:

In each of the steps, write a mathematical formula that responds to the following:

Step 1 Define the mathematical concept in the form of an equation.

Step 2 Illustrate an application of the mathematical concept in the form of an equation.

Step 3 Respond to your classmate's application by reviewing their work and giving your comments.

Step 4 State how this mathematical concept affects people's lives by presenting a text-based explanation and a mathematical equation

Step 5 Cite a variation to the concept through an equation, etc.

Students will broaden and deepen their knowledge on the topic through a cooperative writing exercise based on the above questions.

Imagine: Creative Imaging Exercise

Deepen understanding of the subject matter by taking visual images from web sources and manipulating them with Photoshop to fit explanations about the topic.

Apply sound academic research practice by acknowledging web sources of the images and information students use in their presentations.

Effectively communicate personal insights through visual imagery by using digital graphics tools and multimedia presentations skills.

7

Creating Interactive Games

Introduction

Lesson Objective

- Develop and implement interactive gaming strategies using creative technology.

- Create interactive board and card games relevant to the introduction, exploration, integration, and mastery of any topic.

- Design and execute instructional brochures about the interactive learning games, using Word, Photoshop, PowerPoint.

Skills Learned

- Problem-based web research will stimulate interest and critical thinking about the subject matter and online data gathering.

- Students learn to organize and master subject matter.

- Students will manipulate software in a way that the nature of the program facilitates the creative production process and creates professional-looking learning card games.

Format

The interactive and social nature of gaming and creative production will define the learning process. The first part of the chapter engages students in playing interactive games on-line and developed by the teacher. Students internalize the rules of the games and how these contribute to learning. The second part uses students' current gaming knowledge to conceptualize and develop games based on subject matter. The third part will engage students in designing instructional brochures for their games.

Approach

This chapter increasingly develops students' awareness of both subject matter and interactive gaming strategies. While playing and creating the games, students actively and enjoyably learn about the subject matter and create a fun and dynamic learning environment for themselves.

Tools Needed

- Internet access
- Word, PowerPoint, Photoshop
- Large screen display
- Board paper (colors may be optional), rulers, and pencils

Activity 1, Play: Why Interactive Games Are Relevant To Learning

Objectives

- By playing the game, students and teachers will define key attributes of interactive games.

Class Management

For activities like interactive gaming you will have to define some classroom rules.

1. Students can only play the games in the teacher's list.

2. Students cannot go to any other Web sites except for those that are in the teacher's list.

3. If anyone does not follow the rules, there will be consequences.

- Students and teachers will identify which attributes can be used to bring the same passion for entertainment to learning by playing a game.

Instructions

1 Tell your students that they will be playing interactive electronic games. They will identify the features of games and discuss how the compelling elements can be adapted for learning. Remind your students that only the teacher can choose the games they can will play.

2 Explain to students that they are going to be game critics. The goal is to create criteria to define a good and bad game.

3 Students will play two games and one board game. Following are recommended games for this activity:

  a. Electronic games:

    i. For grades 1–6
- The Sims Series, produced by Electronic Arts,
- Disney Interactive Series, produced by Disney

    ii. For grades 7–12
- Harry Potter Series, produced by Electronic Arts, http://harrypotter.warnerbros.com/home.html
- Civilization 3, created by Sid Meier, produced by Infogrames, http://www.civ3.com

  b. Board and card games:

    i. For grades 1–6
- Monopoly
- Blackjack

    ii. For grades 7–12
- Scrabble
- Pictionary
- Poker

I intentionally did not include learning games in the list. The point of the activity is not to teach students academic content. The activity is designed as a hands-on research-based lesson. Specifically it seeks to engage learners in practical research on the compelling nature of interactive games for K-12 students.

Today's Students, Games, and Learning

By focusing on the similar points, you are able to identify the most common game elements that students respond to. As students recognize that these variables engage their attention, the class will be made aware of the intrinsic nature of their generation vis-à-vis interactive games. Use these variables in designing learning games. You will be amazed at the longer attention span on the subject matter that this process will evoke.

4 For more games, go to any search engine and type key words such as:
  - board games
  - card games
  - interactive games

5 Allow the students to play the games for no more than 15 minutes. Keep reminding them to think of the elements that make them like and not like the games.

6 Divide the class into groups of three. Give each group a 3 x 2-feet worksheet with the above guideline.

7 After students are done responding to the guideline, post these on the board. Make a tally of similar points and keep the other points as part of their findings and conclusions. If your have a projector, type key points in PowerPoint so the whole class can see them. Print copies for each of the students. Tell them to hold on to their copies for the next activity.

Reflections

Review the experience with students. You may ask them the following questions:

Why do you think students like playing interactive games?

GAME	ABOUT THE GAME	
	what you liked	what you didn't like
CIV 3	there were exciting variables I could manipulate	I got confused with the tools

Sample Answers

- We get to manipulate the variables that make us win.
- The story is not final; we write it as we play the game.
- The graphics are awesome.
- The interface responds to what we make it do. We have some level of control.
- We like the fight scenes.
- We like to win.
- Games make us think of alternatives.

  How can the interest in games be transferred to the classroom?

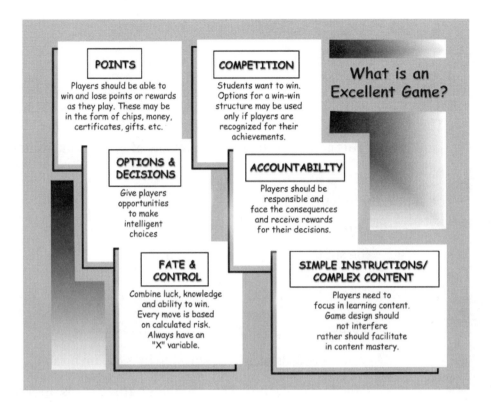

Sample Answers

- We should create activities in class that are as exciting and entertaining as games.

- There should be group competition.

- Graphics helps us to remember subject matter.

- We can make intelligent games.

> The teacher may choose to create a game targeted to the level of the students and the topic of the course.

Summary

- Most games are violent and void of useful knowledge.

- Games keep students' attention longer than traditional classroom activities.

- Games motivate students and are familiar to them. Intelligent games provide students new and hands-on ways to solve problems.

- With technology, teachers and students can create engaging, dynamic, intelligent, and fun content-based games.

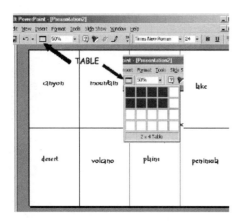

Activity 2, Explore:
Play a Content-Based Card Game

Objectives

The class will play a card game called Memory. The cards are about land forms. This game is intended as a review of the lesson. Students will:

- Learn the rules of the game.
- Socially interact with one another.
- Review the subject matter, which is land forms.

Instructions

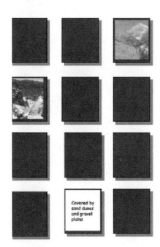

ALL CARDS ARE PLACED UPSIDE DOWN, SIDE BY SIDE, ON THE TABLE.

The goal of each player is to match 3 cards on LAND FORMATIONS.
1 Image
2 Title
3 Text Description
There are 60 cards

In round 1, players have to guess what images and text are under each of the cards.

For every round, each player will open 2 cards, if both cards don't match, she/he cannot open a 3rd card If both cards match, he/she can open a 3rd card.

1   Explain the rules of the game to the students.

Place all cards facing down, side by side, on a table.

The goal of each player is to match three cards on land formations according to:

Image

Title

Text Description

There are 60 cards. The player with the most points and cards wins.

In round one, players have to guess what texts and images are under each of the cards. For every round, each player will open two cards. If both cards match, he can open another one, if not, he cannot open a third card.

Each time a player opens two matching cards, he gets 10 points. However, if he doesn't get the third matching card, he returns all three cards facing down in the same place on the table.

Each time a player opens three matching cards, he gets 15 points. He takes the cards and stacks these in front of him.

2 Divide the class into teams of four and distribute a set of cards for each of the teams. The game isn't finished until a winner is declared.

Reflections

After playing, ask each of the teams what they remember about land forms. Ask them to what they would have remembered if they had been given a list to memorize instead of playing the game.

What were the ups and downs of the game?

Sample answers:

UPs

- By remembering the position of the images, you remember the definitions of the land forms.

- We should repeat cards about the land forms so we can really master the subject matter.

- It was more fun that just having a list and memorizing the definitions.

- Peer competition keeps us paying attention.

DOWNs

- The descriptions of the images are way too long.

- There should be one person who holds on to the answers and acts as the referee.

- Some of my group mates were cheating.

- Some images do not relate to the definition.

Each time a player opens 2 matching cards, he gets 10 points from the bank. However, if he doesn't get the 3rd matching card he returns all 3 cards upside down in the same place on the table.

Each time a player opens 3 matching cards, he gets 15 points from the bank. He/she takes the cards and stacks these in front of him/her on the table.

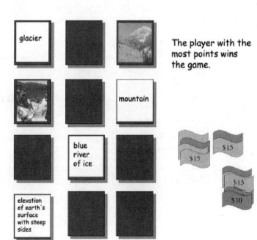

The player with the most points wins the game.

Summary

- Using gaming dynamics to create interaction and competition builds interest in the subject matter.

- With interactive games, subject mastery and reviewing for tests can be fun.

- Time-bound and competitive games raise adrenalin. This then makes us think faster and clearer.

- Games stimulate our desire to win, and students learn and master the subject matter.

Activity 3, Integrate: Creating Content-Based Card Games

Objectives

Developing card games can be tedious if one has to make copies of every picture and manually cut and paste each of these on board paper. The final product tends to look messy and unprofessional. It is expensive and time-consuming as well.

With technology, students and teachers are able to create games targeted to meet subject matter standards and course requirements. Additionally, production standards will be close to industry level and in the long term will not demand as much in creation time and materials costs.

In this activity, students will create an interactive card game and a PowerPoint presentation that explains the rules of the game.

Instructions, Part 1: Writing Rules of a Card Game

1 Divide the class into teams of three. Ask the students to assign a representative to pick from the topics in the box. Instruct the teams to discuss the design and mechanics of their card game. Each of the topics will require students to engage in research from the web or from references in the classroom. Research en-

tails understanding the subject matter and accessing materials such as images, videos, and animation to enhance their presentation of content in the form of a classroom game.

2 Give a brief overview of tools in PowerPoint.

a) Slide Layout options. Choose between a freestyle (choose blank) and a formatted layout design. Go to Format and choose Slide Layout, which will bring up the Slide Layout Pane on the right side of your screen. Choose a slide layout from the drop-down menu. Note the combination of text and image boxes provided in these slide layout designs. You will find the following categories:

 i. Content layouts

 ii. Text and content layouts

 iii. Other layouts

b) Color scheme options. Define colors for consistency in look and style. For example, if you want your presentation to represent the colors of your game, control the preferences provided in the color scheme.

 i. Choose Slide Design from the Slide Pane.

 ii. When you choose one of the designs, the color scheme options appear. Click your choice.

 iii. Click on the triangle in the slide pane and the options are there for you to:
 • Apply to All Slides
 • Apply to Selected Slides

c) Clip art options. These are ready-made pictures to enhance presentations. Depending on the slide design you choose, you may insert clip art in various ways.

 i. Some slide designs already have icons onscreen to access clip art. Click these tools to add clip art.

 ii. Go to Insert, choose Picture and click Clip Art.

Before class begins, make a list of topics that your students can choose from for their game design activity. Type the topics on a sheet of paper, cut these into separate pieces. Fold the pieces of paper and place these in a small box or basket.

Game Step 1

Write Instructions in the Active Voice

Tell students to identify Step numbers as they write their game instructions.

Underline the use of action-oriented phrases or sentences. This is a good opportunity to explain the difference between ACTION-ORIENTED and PASSIVE phrases or sentences in the context of writing instructions.

Game Step 2

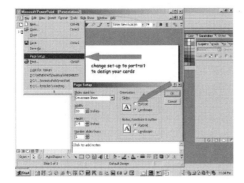

Animation and Presentation Goals

Remind students about the effect of animation in terms of the impact they intend to achieve with their presentations. Tell them to be clear about the Instructional Goal of the presentation.

In most cases, you don't have to show students all the tools and commands. With an overview of the custom animation tools, you will give students a basis to discover how the software works through experimentation.

iii. Choose a category and double-click the image to add it to the slide.

iv. If you want to expand the clip art library, access free clip art downloads on the Microsoft web site or make your own in Photoshop.

d) Custom animation options. You may control the motion and rhythm of images, text, and slides. The slide pane assists in keeping to task by documenting previous choices. Animation options provide visual action tools that transform your slide show into an animated presentation.

   i. Control the mood and style
   Choose from Subtle, Moderate and Exciting options, to create the mood of the presentation.

   ii. Control pace and focus
   Choose from Entrance, Emphasis, Exit, and Motion Path to create action schemes in your slides, objects, and text.

   iii. Insert files from Photoshop
   Go to Insert and choose Picture and a menu of image types appears. Click From File, highlight the file, double-click, and the image will appear. Adjust as you wish by moving the square pegs found on the edges of the image.

   iv. Make animations work. Use the slide pane on the right side of the screen, which guides and records the animation steps you completed. To test individual animation effects, click Play or Slideshow at the bottom of the slide pane.

   v. Rearrange slides. Click the Slide Sorter View icon below the slide layout on the left side of the screen. To change positions, your have two options: click on a slide and drag it to its position, or use the Edit menu to cut and paste.

   vi. Use drawing tools to connect and illustrate instructions. Click AutoShapes in the toolbar and choose any of the

To find shapes, click on the arrow and then choose the shape.

Fill color   Line color

shapes you want to use. Click on your slide, and the shape appears. You can adjust the size by stretching the handlebars. You can also turn the shape by clicking and dragging the green dot. To change line color, click Line Color icon and choose a color. To change the inside color of the shape, click the Fill Color icon and choose from the color options. These icons are normally found in the toolbar.

3   Create playing cards in PowerPoint.

a) Design your card template on 8.5" x 11" board paper. Go to View, choose Master and click on Slide Master. Click the Table icon on the toolbar. Highlight eight squares and two rows.

b) Click the Show Grid icon.

c) Use the gridlines and card sizes defined by the table as your guide in sizing the cards.

d) Increase and decrease size of cards by dragging the black handlebars.

4   Use the PowerPoint tools to insert images and format text in each of the cards.

5   Print the cards and use a cutter or sharp pair of scissors to slice pieces from the slide.

Instructions, Part 2: Play Card Games

There are 3 primary goals for this activity.

- Learn subject content through interactive peer learning.
- Test the playability of the games.
- Build communication skills.

Step Towards Moviemaking

Learning animation tools in MS Powerpoint prepares students for the more complex moviemaking projects.

Game Step 3

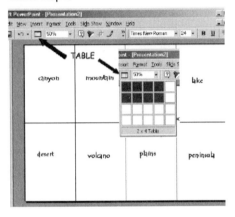

Land forms cards

1 Distribute game feedback sheets to every student. Tell them that the guidelines are based on the class discussion on what makes a good or bad game. They will complete these sheets after playing each of the games. Following is general criteria for the game review:

- What did you learn about the content of the game?
- Was the game fun, entertaining and captivating?
- What could be improved in terms of playability, content, look of the cards, and group facilitation?

2 Have teams send representatives to pick one piece of rolled paper to determine the order of game presentations. Remind teams to designate a PowerPoint presenter and a game facilitators. Team members should be divided equally among the groups.

3 Instruct each team to load their game instructions in presentations on the computer connected to the LCD monitor.

4 As the presenter introduces the game, the facilitators distribute the cards and other materials to their groups. The facilitators continue to help the groups as they play the game.

5 After the game each of the students responds to the Game Review sheet.

A narrow chasm with steep cliff walls, cut into the earth by running water

(www.dictionary.com)

CANYON

TEXT DESCRIPTION

ILLUSTRATION OR PHOTO

NAME OF THE LAND FORM

6 Briefly review the game with the class. Ask students for their highs and lows on the game. Proceed to the next game.

Reflections

After all the groups present their games, review the card game development activity with the class.

- What did you learn about the subject matter from making card games?
- How did interactive games change the classroom environment?
- Was it easy to teach your games to the class? Why? Why not?

Summary

- The process of creating a game was also a process of learning about the subject matter. This time, it was fun and empowering because game design is an interest of Generation Y students.
- While designing a game that includes questions, facts, and images, students will have to know what information about the topic matters and that they can make it relevant and stimulating.
- Teaching fellow students rules of the game builds self-confidence and develops communication skills. Team members need to listen to the instructions of the speaker and make sure the groups understand the steps and rules of the game.

Activity 4, Imagine, Part 1: Creating a Multimedia Game

Objectives

This activity will engage the class in creating interactive classroom games, using still images, text, movies, animated clips, and audio. Further, because of the more sophisticated nature of the game, students will be challenged to invent ways that create dynamic class interaction.

A Problem-Based Game with Multiple Solutions

Instructions

1 Present a sample game, Choices.

Step 1 Divide the class into four groups. Each group creates a community name and elects a senator to represent their interests.

Step 2 The teacher decides on a topic for the day. For example: America's Dilemma with Iraq

Step 3 A question is posed in the beginning of the game.

If you were the president of the U.S., what would you do with Iraq?

Step 4 Information Cards

Each player picks one information card and reads the instruction. These cards help the senator make intelligent responses to the question cards.

Instructions: Require the senator and his or her community to go to the web to look for information about a specific aspect of the issue. In this case it could be, "Find the total number of American soldiers killed since the war against Iraq began."

Information: Include still and video and text with specific data about the issue. In this case it could be a CNN news report.

Step 5 Question Cards

For every turn, a senator must pick one card from this set. The card will contain a question, and the senator should answer the question with a strategy card.

Step 6 Strategy Cards

There are five subsets in the strategy card set: religion, business, political, military, and education and culture. To respond to the question card, the senator will choose one of these cards. Since the cards are face down, the senator may pick a maximum of three cards and choose the best one to respond to the question.

Step 7 Ballot Cards

There are eight types of ballots. Each member of the community receives a set of the eight cards. These cards are responses to the choices made by the senators in each turn. Each positive response card is equivalent to two points, the negative card minus two points, and a neutral card is zero points. Cards remain face down until all ballots are cast.

Response Cards:

1	Will give way to progress	+2
2	Responds to people's needs	+2
3	Respectful of diversity	+2
4	Destructive to the community	–2
5	Tunnel Vision	–2
6	Power-tripper	–2
7	Indecisive	0
8	Procrastinator	0

Step 8 Ballot Count and Judgment

Compute total votes. Depending on the outcome, the scores may result to either one of both:

Good Idea

When total points equal a positive number

Bad Idea

When total points equal a negative number

The winner is the one with the most GOOD IDEA cards.

The loser is the one with the most BAD IDEA cards.

2 Instruct teams to proceed with designing their games. This time, the game is mainly concerned with making decisions on issues about the subject matter.

Information Card

Bush outlined a new rationale for military action, claiming that Iran, Iraq and North Korea were seeking to develop chemical, biological and nuclear weapons. He declared, "By seeking weapons of mass destruction, these regimes pose a grave and growing danger." "States like these," he said, "and their terrorist allies, constitute an axis of evil, arming to threaten the peace of the world."

Question Card

Should America establish its own government after the war or should it immediately call for elections among the Iraqi people?

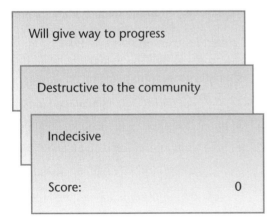

Reflections

While the class plays the games, each individual is given an evaluation sheet to fill with feedback and recommendations. Organize and distribute the sets of responses according to groups. Tell the teams to read the evaluations and note how peers have responded to their interactive games.

Peer Evaluation

- Did you like the game? Why?
- How does playing a game like this enhance or limit your learning about the topic?
- What suggestions do you have to enhance the game?

To distill lessons from this activity, the following questions may be asked:

Plenary Evaluation:

- Did you like designing games? Why?
- What obstacles did you face while creating the game?
- How did you get over these blocks?
- What did you learn in the process of creating the game?
- Why is research on the topic critical in designing a compelling learning game?
- How does a game engage students in learning about a subject matter?

Summary

- Designing a game is much like creating competitive scenarios in a football, hockey, or basketball game.
- In a learning game, designers need to master the subject matter. This necessitates research and mental organization.

- There are three main components to successfully designing a game: knowledge of subject matter, creativity and resourcefulness, and organization.

- When a game is enthralling, you will be able to grab students' attention. They learn about the subject matter and enjoy the process of acquiring and mastering new knowledge.

- Digital media technologies facilitate and enhance the process of research, production, and presentation. Digital tools provide easy access to a database, which makes valuable information and images about the subject matter acccessible. With PowerPoint, one can easily produce and reproduce cards. For example, a master template provides a consistent layout for the cards. With the same software you have the means to present your project in lively ways.

Activity 5, Imagine, Part 2: Packaging the Game

Objectives

This aspect of the lesson provides students with a real world context of game designers. Students look at their projects in the same way as game designers. It is the next big step to selling the product to the marketplace.

GAME	ABOUT THE GAME	
	what you liked	what you didn't like
CIV 3	there were exciting variables I could manipulate	I got confused with the tools

While selling their game to peers, students are mastering the subject matter. With the interactive gaming industry significantly targeting marketing and sales campaigns to Generation Y students, you can imagine how it feels for students to be involved in creating and promoting their own gaming products.

Moreover, by making them aware of the variables involved in designing games, the activity also serves to provide them with the fundamentals of critiquing games sold in the market. Although the students will focus on face-to-face games, the experience initiates them into electronic game design.

Instructions

1 Creating a Brand

   Students define the product and target market. They then create marketing strategies to sell the product to their peers. For example, how does the US-Iraq War Game relate to high school or middle school students? How can the topic be presented to them so that they will buy into the game? On the one hand, while we are talking here of marketing and branding, we are really also relating the topics to day-to-day experiences.

   a) Have the groups write a list of 10 connections that peers may have with their topics. To accomplish this, students will identify reasons that may attract students' attention to their game. Every member of the groups should have a copy of the list.

   Further explain to the students, "When you enter the interactive games section of a store, the range of products on the shelves is overwhelming unless you know what you're looking

Using gaming dynamics to create fun and dynamic peer-to-peer interaction builds interest in mastering the subject matter.

Time-bound activities optimize Youth adrenalin and get students focused on winning and then in the process, learning about the subject matter.

With INTERACTIVE GAMES, subject mastery and reviewing for tests can be fun!

Students are Game PLAYERS And Subject Matter Learners

Supportive team spirit among team members in a competitive learning environment, builds confidence and excitement in playing and then in the process, learning.

Teachers are game Authors and designers.

With DIGITAL MEDIA, the teacher can create his/her own interactive games, targeted to meet his/her subject matter standards and course requirements.

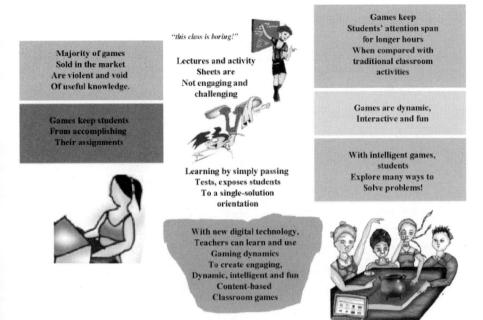

for. Since you're creating a new game, your peers don't know it exists. What is the attraction to the game? Find ways to connect the subject matter to the concerns and experiences of your peers; and make this a must for them to buy."

b) Each of the teams will test their list of 10 from their classmates. They will move around the classroom and independently show the list of 10 to at least five classmates and ask them, "Which one in the list of 10 connections do you think will capture the interest of your peers? Why?"

They mark the best connection chosen by their classmates and write the reasons on the sheet.

c) The teams regroup and share their findings and create:

   i. Title of the game (no more than five words)

   ii. Game description (two or three sentences or phrases)

d) Game Package Cover

Inform the class that they are going to work on the cover of the box of their game.

Tell them they have 3–5 minutes to go to their favorite search engine and choose three sample game covers that are riveting and irresistible. The goal is for their friends to buy the game because of the captivating cover design.

Students discuss the reasons why they think these covers will stimulate sales of a million copies. On a big sheet of paper, they will write the top five reasons and share these with the class.

e) Identify the most common reasons defined by each of the teams. Instruct the class to take note of these variables when they design their game covers.

d) With clear guidelines for branding collectively created by the class, tell the groups to begin their box cover designs. They will divide the following tasks among teammates:

   i. Text: Word

   ii. Graphics: Photoshop

   iii. Layout: PowerPoint

e) Each of the groups present their cover designs to the class. Conduct a secret vote for the most compelling cover designs using these three categories:

   i. Text: Are the words powerful and moving? Do they convince me to buy the game?

   ii. Graphics and images: How effective is the use of the elements of expression in projecting the look and character of the game?

   iii. Layout: Are the images and text creatively and logically organized in a way that the potential customer is not confused where to begin to look? Students can only vote for a group other than theirs. The winning group gets 10 points on their grade for this activity.

2 Writing and Designing A Brochure

  a) The class will be writing and designing a four-page brochure about their game.

  b) Discuss the elements of good and bad brochure designs. In this activity, the brochures will be designed in Photoshop, and text will be developed in Word.

  c) Show sample brochure designs. If you have none, instruct students to find designs in their favorite search engines.

  d) Brochures should include:

    i Content: Title, brief description, key parts, sample images, rules

    ii Creative Composition: a sense of wholeness and continuity in every part

    iii Powerful words and images: convincing and eye-catching words

  e) Instruct each group to print 10 copies of their brochure. They will have to show these copies to various students during breaks and ask them based on what they read and see on the brochure, if they are willing to invest $100 to be a partner and contribute to the development of the game. They should follow up with why they want to or don't want to and then write down their expectations of the game in terms of content and features.

  The form may include questions like:

  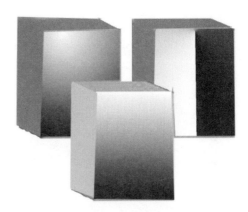

    i. Are you willing to invest $100 to be a partner and contribute to the development of the game?

    _____ yes _____ no _____ maybe

    State your reasons:

    ii. If you decide to join us as a partner, what are your expectations of the game in terms of content and features?

  f) Instruct students to return the completed forms in the next class.

Reflections

Ask students, "What were the most striking things that your friends had to say about the game and investing in your project? What can you conclude about sales possibilities? What matters to your friends?"

Summary

- Preparing a brochure is likened here to the process of capturing key points and writing summaries about the subject matter. Writing a summary is a way to test how much one knows about the subject matter.

- The process of acquiring investments for the game project reflects how much of the subject matter students learned and how they interpreted their learning in the form of a gaming product.

Integrating Games in a Lesson Plan

I would recommend that you use the activities on interactive gaming as part of a bigger lesson plan. Each of the above projects can be more effectively accomplished during longer class periods, designed to compliment other aspects of the lesson.

The level of each activity defined here as Play, Explore, Integrate, and Imagine should match the level of subject matter learning in your lesson. For example, after students design their games, they don't need to present and play these games in one period. You may schedule each game on the day you intend to discuss the topic. The games can be used as an opening, review, or further exploration of subject matter.

From Paper to Video Projects

8

*If a picture is worth a thousand words, then
moving pictures must be worth ten thousand words!*

Lesson Objective

- Learn subject matter through the production of presentations using a digital video camera and user-friendly, non-linear editing systems.

- Create and communicate meaning by combining elements of art and composition and creative technology tools. Integrate writing, visualization techniques, mental organization, sound and music, acting, and camera work into compelling and insightful presentations.

- Gather and organize information into coherent and relevant presentations.

Skills Learned

Students produce both non-fiction and fiction presentations. Non-fiction video lessons reinforce research, experimentation, and the distillation of concepts from concrete data. Fiction presentations focus on developing creative concepts and reinforce knowledge of the essential elements of a story, including plot, conflict, character, setting, and more.

In both these genres, students solve problems and conflicts relevant to their course topics and connect learning to real-life situations.

Format

There are two lesson plans in the chapter. Each lesson plan involves a series of activities integrated into topics relevant to K–12 courses. The end products of these lessons are digital video presentations created by students.

While each of the lessons will be referring to either iMovie or VideoStudio, they are interchangeable.

Approach

The chapter will present lesson plans integrating video into social studies, science, language arts, and media production

The final projects are community-oriented. Students learn about and create projects of value to their various audiences. They are empowered by the opportunity to make a difference as they learn.

Moviemaking Tools are highly effective learning tools. They help students collect and organize information, which in turn facilitates in the formulation of conclusions and articulation of ideas.

Lesson I: Scientific Methodology, the Concept of Change and Moving Pictures

Students create a research video documentary. This lesson teaches students to use iMovie, Photoshop, Word, and either Internet Explorer or Netscape Navigator, as well as a DV camera. Students use the scientific method to research "The Impact of Fast Food Restaurants on Our Bodies." Each of the activities may take 60 to 80 minutes, depending on the pace of the students and the facilities available.

Activity 1, Play: Document Differing Perspectives

Introduction

Many students eat in fast-food restaurants and are not aware of the effect of that kind of food on their bodies.

Objectives

- Learn subject matter through active learning. The activity engages students in recognizing preferred fast-food restaurants and dishes. Students also find out how much these restaurants impact communities all over the world.

- Use the camera for data gathering. Students use the camera, experiment in the use of shots and angles, and develop a set of questions for collecting data.

- Learn non-linear editing for organizing data. Learn basic editing tools in iMovie, which include image capture, cropping, and a timeline to organize their findings into a logical presentation.

- Formulate questions and hypotheses. At the end of the activity, students formulate questions about their findings and feature these in a 30-second digital movie.

- Learn from peers through critical viewing of presentations and discussions. Students watch each other's presentations and form

Problem Solving

By engaging students in a problem solving research activity in the form of a video documentary, teachers connect theoretical learning to real world needs and issues using a camera, non-linear editing software, and a critical and creative series of lessons.

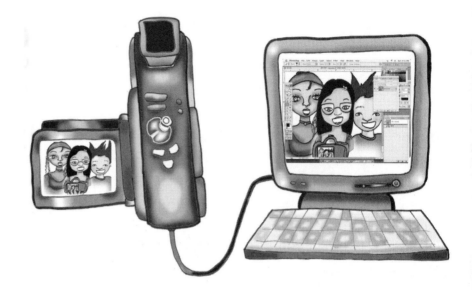

conclusions, which will then become the bases of the next activity, creating a hypothesis.

Instructions

Close up shot, frontal view

1 Tell students they will gather information from peers about their favorite fast-food restaurants.

2 Divide the class into groups of three. Give each group a camera. Each group is tasked to interview all members, and each individual learns to use the camera. The goal is to find one another's favorite restaurant, favorite foods, and frequency of trips to the restaurant.

3 Illustrate various types of camera shots and angles they can use. Each of the groups must use a total of three shots and three angles for all the interviews.

Interview 1

Close-up shot Position the camera frame to fit the face of the interviewee.

Frontal view Position the camera in front of the interviewee.

Interview 2

Medium shot	Focus the camera to frame the interviewee from the waist up.
Low-angle view	Position the camera lower than the face of the person being interviewed.

Interview 3

Long shot	Extend the camera frame to view the whole body with the background visible.
High-angle view	Position the camera on a higher plane than the interviewee.

Medium shot

4 Familiarize students with the basic functions of the camera.

a) Turn the camera on and shift to Camera mode.

b) Open the screen viewer. Place the camera on a tripod so you can keep it stable. If you don't have a tripod, hold the camera with two hands and rest your left elbow on one of your group mates' shoulder for balance and stability.

c) Position your camera according to the prescribed angle and distance. Tell your interviewee to look at the camera as they talk. Keep your eyes on the screen viewer while directing the interviewee.

d) To begin shooting, press and hold the Record button. After she responds to each question, press and release the Record button.

5 Tell students they will interview three students about their favorite fast-food restaurants and meals and make sure that in every interview they use each of the prescribed camera angles and shots.

Long shot, high angle view

I-Movie Clip Length

Make sure your shots do not go more than 9 minutes and 30 seconds, otherwise I-Movie will cut up the scene and create a new clip. To achieve a lively rhythm and pacing in your movies, use shorter clips.

Marking Your Shots

By releasing the Record button on the DV camera, the shot is automatically registered as a clip. It will be easier to edit if you have independently marked clips.

Screen Resolution

When using iMovie, your screen resolution should be at least 800 x 600. If you have a bigger monitor, you may want to increase resolution to 1024 x 768.

Firewire Cable

The smaller plug will be inserted into the camera while the bigger one is inserted into the computer.

Clip Time Code

On the upper left hand of the clip, you will see the time code of a clip. For example, 2:43:12 means the clip is 2 minutes, 43 seconds and 12 frames long.

6 When done, instruct each of the groups to download their interview files onto the computer.

7 Guide them in capturing footage from the camera.

a) Open iMovie. When you open iMovie for the first time, a clap stick will appear on your screen. Click New Project. The iMovie window appears. Note the names of controls.

b) Shift the camera mode to Play (VCR) and connect the camera to the computer. You should see the words "Camera Connected" on your screen.

c) Click the Import button and watch your movie shots come in and position themselves as clips on the shelf. iMovie will detect the beginning and ending of your shots. When all clips are imported, you may turn off your camera. When you do this, the software automatically shifts to Edit mode.

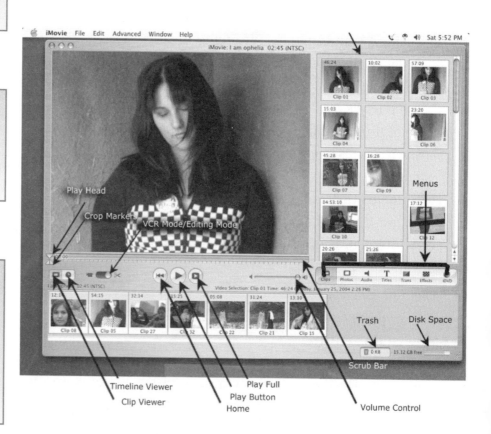

8 Explain to your students that they will begin to organize footage in a logical order depending on the responses they got. The audience should understand the answers to the three questions.

9 Encourage students to review their clips and choose statements that effectively and objectively communicate the message about fast-food restaurants and their peers. Illustrate one way of trimming clips to the class.

a) Select a clip. Note that the first scene appears in the Monitor window. Play the clip.

b) Decide which parts of the footage you wish to keep within the clip. Move your cursor to the Scrubber bar (beneath the triangular handle), and two tiny, transparent, triangular handles appear. Drag the left handle to the beginning of the footage you wish to keep. Then take the right handle to the end of the footage.

The Timeline Is A Multimedia Mental Organization Tool

With a powerful drag-and-drop system, students organize the flow of their interviews according to a logical sequence. Instead of using the traditional paper and pen, they have moving pictures and audio as tools.

Reorganizing Images In The Timeline

Non-linear editing allows moviemakers to cut and paste clips in the Timeline. If you change your mind about the order of the images, you may click on the image/clip and then Cut and Paste or Drag this to another space anywhere on the Timeline.

c) Choose Edit and click Crop. Drag the cropped clip from the shelf onto the timeline.

d) Repeat the process of cropping and dragging of clips to the Timeline until you have all the interviews trimmed and organized.

10 Instruct students to save their project file.

a) Go to File and choose Save Project File.

b) Go to Desktop, create a folder, and name it with the student's name and "fast foods."

11 Tell students to move around the classroom and watch each other's 30-second presentations and have the entire class discuss their findings and come up with a collective conclusion about the subject matter.

Reflections

Prepare to ask questions that will help students critically review the activity. "What did you learn from the process of gathering initial information about the research project?"

Content

Sample Answers

• Many of our friends love fast food restaurants.

• Some were shy but most agreed to speak to the camera.

"What questions come to mind about fast food restaurants and meals based on the initial data gathered?"

Sample Answers

• We wonder why they are so cheap when compared with other types of restaurants.

• Fast food restaurants target students.

"Can you come up with initial conclusions about students and fast foods based on these data?"

Sample Answers

- Students don't really know what ingredients they use in the foods at fast food restaurants.
- There are no real alternatives to fast food restaurants. How can anyone beat their price and taste good?!

Creative Media Techniques

"How do you get people to respond to your questions in front of the camera?"

Sample Answers

- We first talked to them about the project before having them face the camera.
- We had no problem getting people to speak in front of the camera.

"How do the various camera angles and shots affect the interpretation of information?"

Sample Answers

- Close-up shots tend to penetrate the deepest feelings and thoughts of the person on camera.
- When you're below the person, and your camera is facing up, the person looks like she or he's standing on a pedestal.

"How do they impact the way the audience comprehends information on the subject matter?"

Sample Answers

- If your camera is low facing up, then you put your interviewee on a higher plane.
- In a documentary like this, close-ups and medium shots work better for interviews. You can really feel the person talking.
- You can use long shots for showing the facade or adboard signs of the restaurants.

Images And Text Tools Help In Learning

The images and the text combined provide students with creative and powerful tools to present data and formulate their conclusions and hypothesis.

In a sense, this is like teaching a class how to write a five-paragraph essay, only this time students are having fun learning the scientific research methodology and creating a research documentary using moving pictures, text and a video editing Timeline tool.

Video For Data Gathering

"How did the use of video facilitate data gathering and organization of your information?"

Sample Answers

- You can't miss anything a person says. When you take notes of an interview, you tend to forget some of the things the interviewees say. The camera just keeps them complete.
- With a non-linear editing system, you have the timeline and the clips library to help organize your files.
- It's so great to be able to move information from place to place and not have to worry about erasures.

Summary

- People have different perspectives.
- Since we involve people other than the class in the project, we need to be able to convince them of the importance of the project and keep them relaxed in front of the camera.
- It is vital to present the interviewees' point of views in the most objective manner. It helps to conduct preliminary interviews and then based on their initial response, to position the camera in angles and positions that most effectively highlight responses.
- The use of various angles and shots affect the delivery of content. For example, low-angle shots place the interviewee on a higher plane, while high-angle shots make the interviewee seem less powerful. To strongly push the message, camera positions must correlate to the message of each interviewee's perspective on the issue.

Activity 2, Explore: Formulate and Test Questions and a Hypothesis

Objectives

The next two steps are the formulation of questions and a hypothesis of the research project. By involving more of their peers as interviewees, they will get a broader and increasingly complex sense of the issue. Students will form theories based on data from their peers. This activity elevates students' learning abilities to scientific theories.

Instructions

1 Guide your students in the formulation of questions using their initial inquiries. Provide them with a structure of activities to expand their query with peers who participate in formulating questions and hypotheses.

   a) Write down a summary of your findings about the initial data you gathered.

   b) Share these initial findings with three students other than the ones you already interviewed and ask them what questions come to mind.

   c) Discuss the implications of their questions and ask them to come up with a preliminary conclusion about why students like to eat in fast-food restaurants and how the food affects their health.

2 Tell your students that they will use the camera to document findings. They need to bear in mind the effect of the various shots and angles in communicating the points of views of their interviewees. Also, remind your students to use three types of angles for each of the interviewees.

3 Tell students to capture footage in iMovie, the same way they did in the previous activity.

Hypothesis

A hypothesis is a tentative explanation for an observation, phenomenon, or scientific problem that can be tested by further investigation. (The American Heritage® Dictionary of the English Language, Fourth Edition Copyright © 2000 by Houghton Mifflin Company. Published by Houghton Mifflin Company.)

Questions

After gathering initial information, students will formulate specific questions related to their tentative conclusions on the issue: Why are fast food dishes preferred by peer students? How do eating at fast-food restaurants physically affect your peer students?

4 Teach students a second way of editing clips.

a) Select and play a clip from the Clips pane.

b) Determine the footage you wish to keep within a clip. Move your cursor to the Scrubber bar beneath the triangular handle, and two tiny, transparent, triangular handles appear. Drag the left handle to the beginning of the footage and the right handle to a point just before the beginning of the footage you wish to keep.

c) Press the Delete key to remove excess footage.

d) Drag the left handle to the end of the footage you wish to keep and the right handle to the end of the footage.

e) Drag the edited footage clips from the shelf onto the Timeline.

Yellow Bar

As you drag the right tiny triangular clip, the yellow scroll bar marks the footage you are keeping. As soon as you click Crop, all the rest of the footage is thrown into the Trash bin.

Timeline

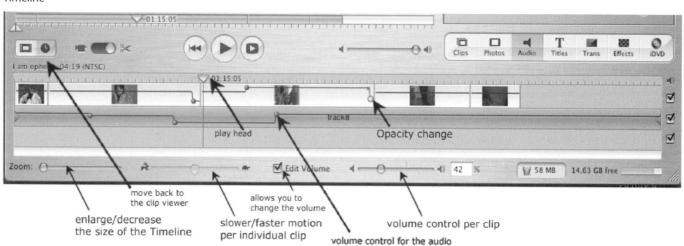

Yellow Bar Beginning

Yellow Bar Center

f) Repeat the process of choosing and deleting footage and dragging clips to the timeline until you have all the interviews trimmed and organized in a logical sequence.

5 Instruct students to save their project file. Each group comes up with a hypothesis and questions from their interviews.

6 Insert a text clip of their questions and hypothesis into the Timeline.

7 Instruct them to click the Title button, and the Title Effects window will appear. Guide them in creating titles with their questions and hypotheses.

a) Choose a Title Effect.

b) Below the choices of Title Effects is a box or two boxes where you type your text. You find a default set of words on these boxes. Highlight them and type your text.

c) Choose an animation effect.

d) Indicate the duration and timing of the animation in each of the text clips.

Title Effects

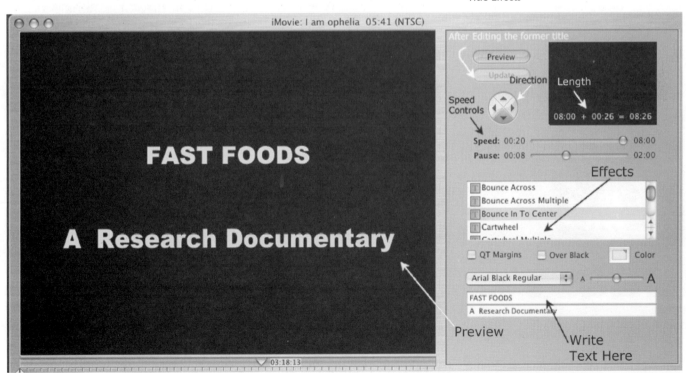

Title Effects Bar

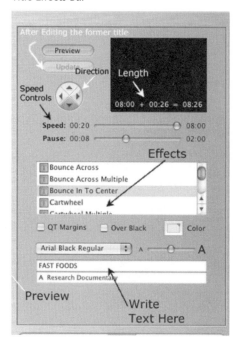

Transitions

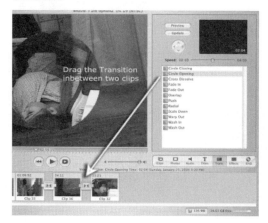

e) Choose between the moving picture clips or plain black as your backgrounds. If you choose black, click on the Over Black checkbox.

f) Choose a color and specify the size of the letters.

8 Remind your students to preview their titles by clicking the Preview button. Precision and mastery of digital tools can only be achieved with constant checking and revising.

9 Instruct your students to organize their titles in relation to the images on the Timeline. Provide them with a mental structure of an effective and creative science research presentation. You may use the following outline as a guide:

Option 1

Title screen:	Title of the presentation
Images Part 1:	Initial findings
Title screen:	Questions
Images Part 2:	Responses to questions
Title screen:	The top three questions
Title screen:	Hypothesis
Images Part 3:	Responses to hypothesis
Title screen:	Group's hypothesis

Option 2

Images Part 1:	Initial findings
Title screen:	Hypothesis
Images Part 2:	Brief insightful quotes
Title screen:	The top three questions
Title screen:	More comprehensive responses
Images Part 3:	Address the hypothesis with findings
Title screen:	Group's hypothesis
Title screen:	Title of the presentation

10 Each group presents their work to the others.

Reflection

Ask your students how images and text tools helped in coming up with questions and developing hypotheses about the subject matter.

Sample Answers

- When you hear your interviewees and see their faces, they are like talking to you and telling you something.

- They don't really tell you the answers to your questions. You need to listen to several and form your own hypothesis.

- Sometimes the interviewees are not even aware that they are helping us find solutions to our queries.

- Text tools create the physical words of a question. Sometimes you're not sure of what you really want to say in the beginning. By seeing these words, you rewrite as you finalize the concept or question in your mind.

Summary

- Using technology tools with peer interviews reinforces the learning of subject matter. Moreover, the technology provides students with easy-to-use tools to document research data.

- Peer collaboration in formulating questions and hypotheses expands the learning experience from a mere theoretical undertaking. It involves students in actively molding conclusions for compelling and real issues that affect their lives on a daily basis.

Activity 3, Integrate: Deepen Subject Matter Analysis

Objectives

Create still images using pictures from the web to present scientific concepts. Students achieve higher learning about the subject matter as well as critical thinking skills:

- Engage in web research to discover the biological effects of fast food meals on the body and to learn about the chemical and biological

Keywords And Web Research

The use of keywords is a fundamental strategy in Web research. It is important for students to determine what words or phrases will lead to relevant information.

Data From Peers

Discovering scientific findings becomes more meaningful when students relate theories with facts gathered from their peers. Moreover, they will be inspired to engage in finding out more about the issue at hand because it is valuable for their peers and correspondingly, to their own lives.

elements that can adversely affect one's health, specifically cholesterol, sugar, and calories.

- Employ image-manipulation techniques to visualize students' findings about the subject matter using Photoshop.
- Integrate still images, text, and audio with video editing software tools.

Instructions

1 Instruct students to search for information on teen health and cholesterol.

2 Tell your students they have one minute to take a cursory look at their search results. They need to list five key words and phrases they deem important to the subject matter, based on the information from the search engine page.

3 Briefly discuss keywords and phrases related to the subject matter, based on what your students gathered from their cursory web search. Begin by asking a volunteer to share one keyword with the class. Then ask the class if anyone has the same keyword. Instruct the volunteer to count how many students had the same keyword. Write the word on the board and beside it, the number of students with the same word. Do this with 10 keywords. If students come up with 10 keywords and fail to raise the most important element of the subject matter, tell your students, "I have a keyword that I deem is important in your research about the subject matter." Then say the word.

4 Assign three keywords to each of the groups. Then tell them to search on these keywords.

5 The goal of each group is to come up with a scientific explanation of how fast foods affect students' health. Give them guidelines to ensure that the research includes important variables such as obesity, hyperactivity, and well-balanced nutrition. Depending on the content standards you intend to meet, you can ask them to get more information that relates to chemical and

biological variables and processes.

6 To organize and present students' ideas:

a) Create a storyboard (a visual outline of the scenes) on paper to visualize your explanation of the concepts in broad strokes and with the use of images.

b) Copy images from the web into Photoshop.

Choose an image on the search engine. Click search option on Pictures or Images. Right click on the image and choose Copy. Minimize your web browser window and open Adobe Photoshop. Go to File, choose New and a dialog box appears. Fill the blanks and click Ok. The picture from the web should appear on your canvass. Make the images screen size to fit the image into the screen size of a video file, go to Image and choose Canvas Size. Change the Canvas Width to 640x480 (NTSC, used in North America) or 768x576 pixels (PAL, used in Europe). Choose RGB color mode.

c) Manipulate images to illustrate the message.

Techniques and tools for image manipulation

i. Make a backup copy of the original file.

ii. Outline a photograph. If the lines are not too thin, choose the Magic Wand. Click at the center part of the line surrounding the image. A Selection Marquee appears. Choose Edit, then Stroke.

iii. Change image colors.

○ You can go from color to black and white. Go to Image, then Mode. Choose Grayscale.

○ You can change color tone. Go to Image, Adjust, then Variations. Click the image above the words as many times as you desire to change the image color. You may use any of these tools to change the hue of the image. Color correct with the Lighten and Darken tools.

Visual Learning

Creative technology involves students in visual learning. For example, time, color, texture, and rhythm can serve the parallel purposes as written explanations of cause and effect. For most students, it takes less effort to understand and remember a theoretical explanation if done as a visually dynamic activity. Additionally, with a hands-on pedagogy students have much more lasting retention levels after they have performed a visual application of the theory.

Naming clips

Title Preview

- Adjust Brightness and Contrast. Go to Image, Adjust, then Brightness and Contrast. Experiment by moving the triangles right and left.

- You can change colors of specific parts of the image. Choose the Polygonal Lasso tool. Move the cursor to outline the edges of the part of the image you want to change. In small increments, click and drag the Polygonal Lasso tool over again to form the shape around the part. Double-click to connect the beginning and end points of the lasso. A selection marquee will appear. Go to Image, Adjust, then Hue and Saturation. Move the triangles to adjust hue and saturation. Click OK when done.

iv. Adjust image texture. Go to Filter and experiment. You may also experiment with the lighting effects. Click Render and try any of the tools.

7 Save all the still images in the movie folder on the Desktop by creating another folder titled Still Images and save the files with numbered titles, for example, part4-1, part4-2, etc.

8 Bring your still image files into iMovie by going to File, then Import File. Navigate to the Desktop, where you saved your files in the folder marked Still Images. Double-click on the individual file and its icon appears in either the shelf or the movie track (depending on the settings of your preferences).

The still image is just like a movie clip. You can click to view this on the monitor window, drag it into the movie track, or incorporate it with a title effect.

9 Add the still images to the first two parts of the video presentation.

   a) Indicate timing of the pictures. Click on a still image clip. Note the minutes:seconds:frames in the duration box. Double-click the number you want to change, type the new number, and press Enter.

   b) Organize images in the Timeline. Drag and drop images according to the order of the explanation.

   c) Add text effects to the images either within the clips. Or you can add new clips.

10 Add audio to the still images. All new Apple computers have built-in microphones. Guide the students in audio recording.

   a) Make sure you test the timing of your scripts by narrating while playing images. Keep your script in front of you and speak loudly into the microphone.

   b) One other team member should control the audio interface while the other speaks. For the audio controller, click the musical note tab on the left side of the Timeline.

   c) Drag the playhead to the beginning of the scene where you want audio added.

   d) Choose the Audio button, click Record Voice, and recite your script. The audio controller should watch the video play as the reader narrates.

   e) When done narrating, click the audio controller to Stop. Listen to the voice recording by dragging the playhead to the spot where you began recording. If it does not sound good enough, delete the audio clip, which is represented as a stripe. Repeat the audio recording and speak closer to the microphone.

11 Review your images, audio, and text. Revise and enhance as needed.

Mental Organization

Saving and organizing projects in digital folders is a way of training students about numerical and alphabetical file structuring. By constantly reminding students to save their projects, the teacher is also teaching them to keep track of their classwork and take accountability for their steps.

Weather Report

For a better appreciation of the integration of graphic images into a video presentation, encourage your students to watch the weather report on television.

Image Effects

12 Save your file.

13 All groups go around and view the work of their classmates.

Reflections

Based on what they experienced in Activity 3, ask each of the groups to identify three highs and lows and how they could improve on the activity for the future.

Sample Answers

Highs	Lows	Improvements
There are many different ways to edit with iMovie.	Sometimes the software doesn't follow the command.	Just do it again; the software has its moods.
I can get my ideas more organized once I see them as linked images.	I can't do all the kinds of effects I want.	Move on to a more complex software like Final Cut Pro.
It's great to have the tools to create a documentary just like what we see on TV.	I don't have a Mac at home; I can't use this software after school.	You have a choice: work, save, and buy a Mac or use a PC program like VideoStudio or Pinnacle Studio.

Before each of the groups share, ask them to look at their peers' input and choose the three most helpful comments for improving their work in the future. Give your students five minutes.

After the discussion, encourage your students to share the three items they wrote with the whole class.

Summary

- Creatively used and organized visual images are helpful in explaining concepts.

- With powerful graphics software one can manipulate web or hand-drawn images to reflect any concept or scientific process.

- Manipulating and organizing visual images is a multiple-intelligence learning strategy. For example, students learn because they visually remember when they altered the color and size of an image to reflect an object's reaction to fatty acids.

- Organizing images in the timeline becomes a way of structuring ideas and scientific research into logical sequences.

- The degree of output reflects the various levels of the students.

> **Voice Recording**
>
> The audio controller must watch the level meter. The audio must reach above the horizontal track. Otherwise, the voice level will be too low and will be drowned by the audio DV recorder track.

Activity 4, Imagine: Community-Oriented Research

Objectives

- Create real-world alternatives to fast food meals. After presenting an analysis on how peers are affected biologically and chemically by fast food, the groups will conceptualize affordable alternatives that will keep peers healthy and happy.

- The alternatives will include a convincing peer-oriented video documentary accompanied by recipes for meals of healthy non-fat food at affordable price.

- Target the alternative to an audience and connect classroom learning to the real world. To convince the audience of the alternatives, they need to research alternative recipes that are attractive to students. These must taste good enough to win over their peers. To convince the market, students should test these recipes, by cooking them either in the classroom or at home and by conducting a taste test among their classmates.

- Use video as a medium of learning, communication, and change. All of the previous points are included in the research-based video documentary project. The presentation is created to convince students to shift to good alternative meals for their own sakes.

> Writing and reading narration is an effective way of reviewing and identifying critical steps as well as highlighting key elements of the subject matter.

Analytical Descriptions

Writing descriptions with the intention of convincing peers about a healthy alternative lifestyle is an exercise in persuasive writing and communications. This time students' inspiration comes from making a difference in the lives of their peers.

Facing Up To Your Market

Peer response drives students to write more clearly. Peer pressure in this case contributes to achieving higher learning goals.

Theory, Reality And Students As Research Scientists

Critical learning is achieved when students are able to relate theory with reality.

Proactive learning is achieved when students proceed with defining alternatives to solve problems based on their research and theoretical formulations.

Instructions, Part 1: Be Proactive: Research the Alternative

1 Using the web as a primary resource, students find alternative delicious and affordable dishes for their peers. They choose an alternative recipe for each of the top five favorite fast food dishes defined by their friends.

2 Students create a fast food product plan that includes five main meals, drinks, and desserts.

3 Each of the groups writes enticing descriptions of each of their food products in no more than three sentences. They must describe why the meal is excellent for their peers' health and enjoyment. They should also write a title of no more than two words for each of the food products.

4 Market Test. Students post these product plans on the walls. Distribute three stars to each student. Instruct them to vote on the best food product from among the meals presented on the board, by sticking one of their three stars beside the meal title.

Voting is an indicator of what may or may not sell to today's generation.

For the next meeting, each of the groups discuss preparations, contributions, and responsibilities for food ingredients for the winning recipe from among the five alternatives.

Instructions, Part 2: Taste of the Alternative

1 Each group cooks their recipe in the school kitchen. If there is no kitchen, they may perform this activity at home and document the process and findings with a DV camera. After cooking, each of the groups conducts a taste test to see how their peers respond to the alternative dish.

2 Since the room will be quite noisy, there is no live narrator activity in this portion. Students do have to document the spontaneous verbal responses of peers upon tasting their alternative meal.

3 Camera shots and angles. Remind the groups about the significance of camera shots and angles as they shoot the cooking portion of the research video documentary. They have to present the ingredients and method of cooking that determine the food's quality and taste.

4 Instruct students to capture their footage into iMovie and edit the clips in logical order. The purpose of the research is to present the ingredients and nutrition information of the alternative meal.

5 At the same time they are editing the clips, the other team member will lay out a menu plan in Photoshop. They will integrate this plan into their video.

6 Remind your students to save their files when done.

Instructions, Part 3: Formulating the Conclusion and Packaging the Video Documentary

1 Groups will present their unfinished video presentations to the class. Afterwards, the class will be asked to respond to the alternative dish presented by each team. Teams will document these responses with their DV camera.

2 Finally, the groups formulate their own conclusion addressed to their peers. They decide how they will present the conclusion as the culmination of their documentary video presentation.

3 They work on the ending part of the video and organize the files in iMovie.

4 They record the narration and merge audio with video.

5 Music in video documentaries. You will engage the class in a brief music sensitivity activity to prepare them for a discussion about music and its emotional role in video presentations. Tell them to close their eyes and to listen to slices of music. When you finish playing each song, pause and tell the class, "Describe the rhythm, sound and texture of the musical piece you heard.

Preparing A CD Copy

Bring five types of musical pieces. Make sure they are of various tempos and texture. You may tape one-minute cuts of each of the songs with a CD burner so that you don't have to change CDs as you conduct the activity in the classroom.

Audio

Music Score

A musical score emotionally accentuates the message of a video presentation. The use of rhythm and sound greatly affect the way the message is communicated. Emotional impact contributes to knowledge retention.

From CD To AIFF File

As iMovie records the song into the Timeline, it concurrently converts this musical piece into an AIFF (Audio Interchange File Format) file.

What feelings does the music emote? What memories does the music bring back to you?"

After all the songs have been played, involve the class in a discussion about music and its function in video documentaries. Sum up the discussion by outlining ways in which music can emotionally underscore and highlight the messages of their presentations.

6 Ask the class to review their presentations and identify parts they can enhance with music to create stronger emotional impact. Each group discusses music titles that they can use as musical scores for their video documentary. They can check iTunes for choices. They can also check search engines for royalty-free music. If they can't find what they want in the music directory, they can use music CDs.

7 To capture music from CDs into iMovie, students can follow these instructions:

a) Go to the Audio palette and insert the music CD into the CD drive. Wait for a few seconds. The list of songs as Track 1, Track 2, etc. will appear on the palette.

b) To play a song, click the track number and the Play button on the palette.

c) To merge the music with your video presentation, drag the track number into the audio track on the timeline. Adjust to the beginning and end of the song as you hear the music played while watching the video.

If you wish to get only a portion of the song, play the piece and then crop at the portion you wish to use.

d) To adjust sound levels and make sure the music does not drown out the narration, click Adjust Sound and drag the purple rubber lines up (louder) or down (softer).

8 Class Presentations. Groups take turns in showing the class their final product. Fellow students give their feedback along the following lines:

a) I liked it because

b) Your group may consider *(provide 1-2 suggested revisions)*

c) By watching your video, I learned *(What's the message of the video presentation?)*

9 Give your constructive feedback to enhance the presentations. Then give the students one more class session to work on revisions.

Movie to computer

10 Convert iMovie files into QuickTime movies. Guide your students with the following instructions:

a) Go to File and choose Export Movie. The Export Movie dialog box appears. On the menu, it says, "Export to." Click QuickTime. In the Formats menu, choose CD-Rom Movie, Medium. Click OK.

b) Type a name for your movie. If you intend to play the movie on Windows, add .mov to the file format. Click Save.

Part 4: Presenting to the Community

1 Organize a video documentary presentation date with students as the audience. Invite other teachers, school administrators, and parents to the event.

2 Instruct each of the groups to prepare a two-minute oral introduction for their presentation. This should include:
   a) Welcoming the audience
   b) Reasons why they worked on the presentation
   c) What they learned as video documentary producers in terms of the subject matter, creative technology, and teamwork.

3 Students present their research documentaries on a large screen with an LCD projector hooked up to the computer.

4 After the presentations, the students conduct an open forum with the audience on the issue and the documentary.

5 Conclude the forum and thank the audience for coming.

Reflections

After the class produced the research video documentaries and presented these to an audience, discuss the following with your students:

"What were your highs and lows about the production process? What did you feel good and what didn't you feel good about?"

Highs	Lows
I liked editing because the tools are easy to use, and I could see the presentation coming together.	Some of the moving images we shot were not well lighted.
I loved the audience responses.	If we had more time we could achieve so much more with the camera shoots.

How did making a movie make you learn about the subject matter? What aspect of the topic made an impact on you?

Sample Answers

- I learned about how terrible fast foods are. I also learned about the various unhealthy and healthy food ingredients.

- In the fast food business, the company makes a lot of money because they prepare food in bulk quantities.

"What would you have improved if you were given another opportunity to work on the project?"

Sample Answers

- Shooting images—I will be more conscious about controlling camera angles.

- Voice levels—I will make sure we wear earphones to listen to the audio quality while doing the shoot.

Summary

- The process of creating video involved three important learning components: dynamic use of technology, creative pedagogy, and peer-to-peer learning. The process evolved from simple to complex activities. Each step is built on previous steps, so that students are increasingly confident and empowered by achieving the fundamental components of the lesson.

- Having an audience watch the videos at the end of the lesson gets students to take accountability for the final outcome of their presentations. The audience and the response of classmates provide positive pressure, one that drives students to raise the standards of their presentations. In the process, students use research, data organization, and critical analysis to achieve subject matter mastery.

- Students use a powerful multimedia format to discuss and promote alternatives to an issue that affects community health.

Lesson II, Fiction Moviemaking: A Story Comes to Life

Students will create a fiction movie. This lesson teaches students Ulead VideoStudio, Adobe Photoshop, and Microsoft Word. The series of activities provides teachers with strategies for producing fiction stories with multimedia tools, peer-to-peer learning, and exploration of the elements of creative expression.

Students generate ideas and develop storylines using sensory and hands-on exercises. Art elements, such as as clay and other materials, are integrated into the video expression.

Depending on the education standards for the class as determined by the teacher, the lesson can be expanded to meet language learning goals, utilize creative literary devices, and apply creative thinking to the theme and story.

Activity 1, Play: Waking Up the Senses

Objectives

- Awaken senses with objects of various textures.

- Expand vocabulary by describing the textures using descriptive words.

- Introduce the concept of metaphors by linking descriptive words to emotions and experiences.

- Write personal narratives through a free writing exercise, stimulated by the sensory-emotions-memory activities.

Instructions

First Round: Sensory Perception and the Elements of Art

1 Instruct students to go out of the classroom and bring back three objects with a variety of textures.

2 Divide the class into groups of five. Instruct each of the groups

to form a circle seated on the floor and to place their objects at the center.

3 Each group member should have a pen and paper. They begin with an individual volunteer who takes one of the objects and feels its texture. The volunteer describes the object to the group using three adjectives.

4 Group members write the adjectives on their sheet of paper.

5 The person to the left of the first volunteer continues the activity by taking another object from the center and describing its texture and color with three adjectives. The next person follows, until all group members complete the round.

Second Round: Sensory Perception and Emotion

1 This time, the first volunteer takes another object and describes it by connecting the adjectives with an emotion. For example, the student may say, "This rock is rough on my hands; it feels edgy. The handkerchief is so soft; it feels warm and fuzzy. The ball pen is smooth and slimy; it feels like it may just slip away."

2 The person to the left of the first volunteer continues the activity by taking another object from the center and describing it by connecting the adjectives with an emotion. The next person follows and so on until all group members complete the round.

3 Group members write the adjectives and emotions on their sheet of paper.

Third Round: Sensory Perception and a Memory

1 Another volunteer takes an object and thinks of a memory that relates to the object. For example, the student may say, "The dry branches remind me of the winter day when my brothers, sisters, and I walked in the forest by ourselves. I was only eight then and was firmly holding my sister's hand. The dry branches were all over the place; we even stepped on them."

2 The person to the left of the first volunteer continues the activ-

ity by taking another object and then relating this to a memory in his or her life. The next person follows and so on until all group members complete the round.

Fourth Round: Sensory Perception and A Moment in Life

1   Students take an object, describe its features by how it feels, relate this to an emotion, and connect it to a memory. Encourage your students to include adjectives from other sensory stimuli, for example, hearing, taste, and smell.

  They will write with Word. When they run out of words to use, they can go to Tools, Language, then Thesaurus. When a red or green line appears, they highlight the word and go to Tools, then Spelling and Grammar. A dialog box appears and they will find out Word's comments on their grammar. If they agree, they click OK.

2   Give students 10 minutes to write.

3   The groups form a circle and read each other's stories.

Reflections

Review the four steps and ask the groups to reflect and derive lessons from the activity.

"What did you think of the activity?"

Sample Answers

- It was cool, the stories we came up with were all different.

- I couldn't have imagined coming up with this story.

"How does the process of word listing stimulated by sensory perceptions, such as touch and sight, help in writing?"

Sample Answer

- The list came from one's sensory reaction to the objects. It was easier to come up with descriptions when you're describing a reaction from an experience.

"What did you think of each other's stories in the end?"

Sample Answer

- Far-out! I learned stuff about my classmates that I never knew before.

More questions to guide your critical discussions: "What was the most difficult obstacle to overcome in writing? How did word brainstorming help in your writing? How did the tools in Word enhance your writing process?"

Summary

- Sensory stimuli make students more sensitive and observant about how the world shapes their lives.
- Word brainstorming is a very useful springboard to writing. Students come up with the initial words and their vocabularies are expanded with the use of Word's thesaurus and by listening to other students' words. Also, the grammar and spelling tool flags errors in writing and offers suggestions for revision.
- Sharing writing with peers inspires students to write more conscientiously and sensibly. It makes such an impact on one's sense of self when writers hear their own voices.

Activity 2, Explore: Storyboard to Storyline

Objectives

- Tap into personal experiences as content for developing and writing stories.
- Apply the previous activity lessons in writing: the use of concrete descriptions, the use of metaphors and analogies, and creating word banks for developing stories into meaningful, beautifully-written fiction storylines.

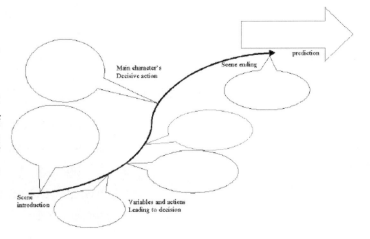

- Explore VideoStudio as a means to edit, organize, and present storylines.
- Work as partners, assisting each other by sharing ideas and exploring VideoStudio.

Instructions

1 Share and analyze storylines. Tell students to choose striking elements from the personal stories shared in their groups. Describe a striking element by giving them examples.

- When people close to you change their ways: "I realized my parents were no longer talking to each other for many nights. Dad came home later in the evenings and left us to have supper by ourselves. Mom was quiet when we asked about Dad. It felt weird. Home life changed."

- When you unexpectedly got into trouble: "My friends all took a sip except me. I didn't even know what tequila was except for the fact that it was alcohol and that it was one of those prohibited substances in school. I turned red with shame and after all the insulting remarks from my friends, I agreed to drink—but I just pretended that I did. As soon as I held the bottle, I heard the teacher's voice. He was calling my name."

- When someone did something funny and ridiculous: "The poetry reading began. I was about to read my piece when I heard my friend Jose giggle and say "Oh!" and giggle again. My poem started with the word "Oh!" and had lots of these "Ohs." As I started to read I couldn't help myself from laughing. My friend laughed, the class laughed. The teacher was not at all laughing in the beginning. I was getting nervous. She surprised me most when she got infected with our laughter too.

2 Instruct the groups to discuss the above elements and pinpoint reasons why they strike a memory chord.

3 With the whole class, ask the groups to share the reasons why the story elements struck them. Briefly discuss the elements of a good storyline with the class:

   b) An action-oriented plot driven by characters that keeps readers on the edge.

   c) Relevant issues that audiences relate to.

   d) Emotional experiences and events that connect to the audiences' sensibilities, such as humor, fear, peer pressure, and turning points.

4 Create a storyline with tableaus. Divide the class into groups of two. They each choose one main character from their own stories. The partners are given a multi-colored set of clay. They create the following tableaus with 3D characters molded with clay, integrating the elements of a good story:

   Scene 1   An unforgettable moment in the main character's life.

   Scene 2   The main character's ultimate dream or wish

   Scene 3   An obstacle that prevents the main character from achieving his or her dream or wish

   Scene 4   What the character will do to achieve the dream; other characters who can help the main character

   Scene 5   Struggles the character needs to go through to achieve the dream

   Scene 6   What happens to the character at the end of the unforgettable moment

5 Prepare the class to write narratives for their unforgettable life moments.

   a) Open a new Word document. This is a narrative writing activity; you are writing your stories.

   b) Use your clay tableaus as a guide in writing your story. Following are writing rules that will enable you to write without fear and overcome writer's block.

   • Don't worry about spelling, punctuation, or grammar.

   • Focus on the details: the colors and textures of a wall,

whether the sun was shining, the mood of the character, the unfolding of events, and character responses vis-à-vis various contexts.

d) Write how you feel about this unforgettable incident.

e) You may choose to write in complete sentences, phrases, or words.

6 Partners individually write about the story based on their tableaus. The partner whose story is being told writes in the first person, and the other in the second person.

7 Give the class 10 minutes to write their narratives. Help them describe details, such as: "Don't just say 'house,' describe the furniture in the room."

8 After 10 minutes tell the class to finish writing their last sentence.

9 Instruct partners to read their stories to each other. Explain that they will tell the story with the tableau images in mind. It will be like a slide show. Partners will need to merge the best lines of their narratives into a single narrative. Encourage them to use adjectives, analogies, and metaphors to expound on and enhance their narratives. They have 10 minutes.

10 Guide them on how to shoot each of their tableaus with a DV camera. Encourage your students to experiment with a variety of camera angles and shots.

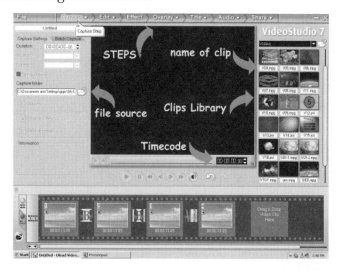

11 Guide them in how to capture images from the camera to VideoStudio.

   a) Open VideoStudio. Connect the camera to the computer through a Firewire cable.

   b) Create a New Project file. Click the Rewind button below the Preview screen to bring back the tape on the camera to the beginning of your first clip.

   c) Capture your footage. As soon as you get to the first part of your clip, go to Capture. The settings on your screen will automatically shift to the Capture interface.

   d) Click Capture Video. When all the clips are transferred, click Stop Capture or press Esc.

12 Introduce VideoStudio to the class.

   a) Review your clips and make sure all of them were captured. Double-click the image in the Library to view this on the Preview Screen. Note how VideoStudio organized your footage into clips in the Library. Each of these clips began when you pressed the Record button and ended when you released the Record button during your shoot.

   b) Go to File, then Preferences. Uncheck "Use default transition effect" and click OK.

   c) Edit your clips. Go to Edit Step. The settings on your screen will shift to the Edit interface. Double-click on an image in the Library and view this on the Preview screen.
   Choose your preferred footage. Click and drag the trim handles to the beginning (left) and ending (right) positions of your choice. Play the selected footage. Hold down Shift key and click Play Clip. If you are satisfied with your choice, click Save Trimmed Video.

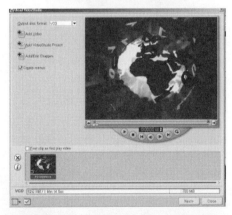

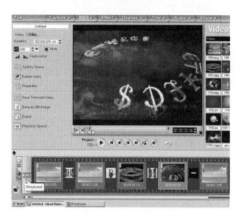

d) Organize each of your clips in horizontal order based on the flow of your narrative. Click, drag, and drop each of the clips to the Timeline.

e) Save your file with the file name containing the student's name and "Fiction."

13 Instruct your students to share their storyboard presentations to at least three sets of partners in the class. They will read the storyline as they share their edited storyboard. Ask them to respond to the following questions and to write valuable suggestions from their classmates on their notebooks.

a) What do you think of the storyboard and narrative?

b) What message do you get from the presentation?

c) Do you have suggestions on how we can enhance the delivery of the message in terms of story structure, character development, and narrative?

Reflections

Review the activity with the class and instruct the partners to discuss the highs and lows of their writing and storyboarding experiences and to write these down in bullet points on their notebooks.

Sample Answers

Highs	Lows
I didn't quite know in the beginning what would come out of the sensory activity. But when I was writing my story, I was surprised how much came out of my mind and emotions.	I had difficulty writing about my experiences.

Summary

- Personal experiences provide a rich resource for writing by offering insight into human life and character.

- Good writing is easier to accomplish with a word bank and a list of metaphors and analogies.

- VideoStudio provides an easy-to-use interface for content organization, specifically in an activity such as creating a narrative storyboard.

- By working with a partner, students are able to build and support each other's ideas. This is especially useful in an activity such as storyline and storyboard development.

Activity 3, Integrate: Dialogue, Character and Video Shoots

Objectives

- Transform personal stories into fiction using literary techniques and the most affective portions of students' stories.

- Write a fiction story and integrate metaphors, analogies, and new vocabulary in their screenplays. Guided by a storyboard structure, construct the narratives in a video script mode.

- Use the DV camera and microphones for video shoots. Use VideoStudio to cut and organize video clips scene by scene into the Timeline and integrate audio clips with the dialogues.

Instructions

1 Guide the class in transforming their personal stories into scripts.

   a) Change the identities of the main characters. Give them different names, addresses and change their professions. The changes should enhance your story and not remove the essence of your message. Give students 10 to 15 minutes.

b) Review the creative elements and flow of your story and add creative elements that will spice up the plot, characters, conflict, and setting. Give students 10 to 15 minutes.

2 With two volunteers, read a part of a sample narrative script with dialogues.

3 Discuss the added value of dialogue in a narrative presentation. It keeps the presentation alive, enriches audio texture, and provides a better sense of the characters.

4 Ask the partners to review their stories and to use Word to insert dialogues and transform the narratives into a script format. Remind them to limit the number of pages to three, as this can be the equivalent of five to six minutes in a video presentation. It may help to show students a one-page sample of a popular movie script.

Clip #	Setting	Character	Narration/Dialogue	Video Images
01				
02				
03				

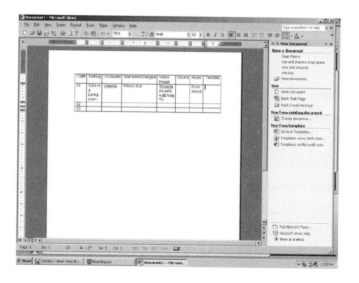

a) Click the Table icon on the task bar and highlight six columns and rows and type the following categories:

b) Use the table as a guide in transforming your narratives into script format. Fill the blanks.

5 **Pre-Production**

Each of the partners has to accomplish the following to prepare for their video shoots:

a) Choose and negotiate with classmate-actors.

b) Improvise costumes and props with available materials in school and at home.

c) Identify settings and improvise with available furniture.

d) Make copies of the scripts for the actors to review, memorize, and prepare for the shoot.

e) Stripe the DV tape. Put a new blank tape in the camera, shift to Camera mode, keep the lens covered, and press Record. By doing this before shooting, you avoid frame dropouts.

f) Finalize the storyboard, shooting sequence, and schedule.

g) If need be, improvise with lights to produce mood effects.

6 **Production**

a) Read the script with the characters. Provide them with an overview of the shooting schedule and expectations. For example, in the first class period, you will shoot five scenes, and you expect your actors to read, memorize, and practice their lines before each take.

b) For every scene, arrange the setting, improvise costumes and make-up, help your actors get ready, and provide relevant information about the characters with reference to the scene.

c) In the beginning of each scene, identify the clip with a white paper background and a scene or sequence number. When you edit the scenes later, the number identification is your guide.

Pre-production

Pre-production involves writing the script, visualizing scenes by sketching them on a storyboard, and creating a production schedule for shooting scenes.

Adobe Premiere 5.0 Classroom in a Book, Adobe Creative Team, 1998, Adobe Systems Inc.

Production

Production involves shooting footage, directing actors, implementing scene and lighting designs, and recording dialogue.

Improvisation

Encourage your students to expand their imagination and avoid spending too much money to create sets, costumes, and props. Use available objects and furniture and clothes from the thrift shop. Students can also use bed linens and covers and reconfigure these according to unique character and scene needs. They can design their own lighting systems by forming cones out of boxes and inserting aluminum foil to increase lighting power.

Post-Production

Post-Production involves capturing tape to the non-linear editing system, editing and organizing scenes, integrating music and narration, and cleaning and fixing scenes.

d) You may engage in many more techniques through experimentation. Be well aware that the angles and distance from the camera is in itself a way to present the message. Do at least three takes per scene. You will want to have a choice of the best shot when you edit. Use the screen viewer as your shooting parameter guide.

e) For dialogues, make sure you may want to use boom microphones. Cameras have built-in microphones but these are not as powerful as boom microphones.

f) To facilitate the process of editing, one of the partner-moviemakers will document each take and place a check mark on the preferred clip.

7 Post-production

a) Capture video files from the camera five scenes at a time. (You don't want to overload your hard drive.)

b) Edit your clips per scene. Go to Edit Step. Switch to timeline mode and organize your edited clips horizontally below the storyboard. Use the storyboard as guide to organizing clips. Work on five scenes at a time. When these have been cut and positioned on the timeline, delete unwanted clips and capture the next set of five scenes.

c) Record the narration. Go to the Audio Step and in the drop down menu, choose Voiceover. Move the jog bar to the part of the scene where the narration should be placed. Click Record Voice and adjust volume accordingly. Click Start and read the narration.

d) Stop the narration. Click Stop Recording Voice or press Esc.

e) Vertically link the narration to the dialogue audio. Cut the dialogue audio clips as you would a video clip. Insert the narration to the voice track guided by the script. Make sure the audio line is directly below the clips they refer to.

f) Save your project file and present this draft to the class.

Activity 4, Imagine Creativity Logic Applied in a Video Presentation

Objectives

- Narrate stories and communicate ideas and feelings through the creative use of the elements of composition, movie titles, and musical score.

- Use VideoStudio to apply movie titles and musical score in the video narrative.

- Present movie narratives to an invited community and engage the audience in a constructive discussion about the stories and presentations.

Instructions

1 Create and insert titles. Guide your students to use title tools and apply these according to the needs of their video presentations.

a) Go to the Title Step. The software automatically shifts to the Title menu. In the Title menu, you create titles on black. If you want the titles over video images, you use the Overlay Step.

b) Create title over black background. Position the jog bar in the place where you intend to place the title. Click on any of the sample titles in the Library.

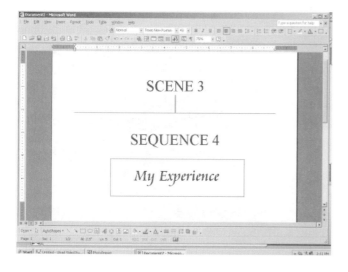

c) Type your title as you would in a Word document. On the left hand of the screen, you can choose font types, sizes, and screen position. If you want title effects, you may click on Border, Shadow, then Transparency. Choose border and shadow effects accordingly.

d) Animate your titles. After working on all the titles, click on Animation. Use any of the animation effects judiciously and with a clear sense of unity in composition.

2 Create scene transition effects. Guide your students to use the effect tools according to the needs of their video presentations. Remind them to limit the use of transition effects to two types in order to keep a unified aesthetic look.

a) Go to the Effect Step. Click on the inverted green triangle to open the library of transition effects.

b) Try all the effects and choose the one that best fits the tempo, mood, and overall message of the video presentation.

c) Drag and drop the transition effect between two clips in the Timeline.

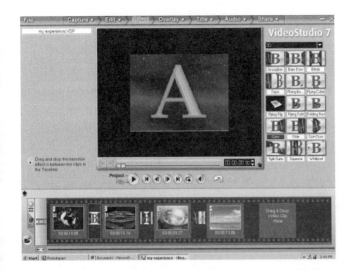

3 Integrate a musical score. Guide your students to use the music scoring tools according to the needs of their video presentations. There are several ways of scoring in VideoStudio. They can use the music clips in the Library or bring in MPEG or CD files. Combining music clips can be tricky with the use of the voice track for the narration.

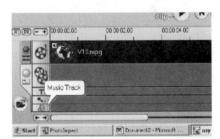

a) Use music clips in the Library. Drag and drop a clip in the music track. Using the yellow trim handles select the music you wish to keep. To see the end of the clip, choose the Fit Project in Window option for the timeline.

b) Cut and move the clip in its space in relation to the video and voice clips. You may also use the time code. Click the triangle facing up to extend the clip and the triangle facing down to shorten the clip.

c) You may also use the fade in and fade out options at the beginning and end of each clip.

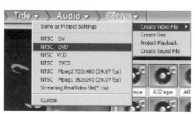

d) To adjust volume, click Clip Volume and adjust accordingly.

4 Remind students to save their project files at all times, especially when they are done.

5 Tell your students that for the community presentation they will save their files on a CD or DVD in video format.

   a) Go to the Share Step and choose Create Video File.

   b) Click on your file output. Write your filename and choose the MPEG file format.

6 Partners present their work to the class. The class gives feedback. Give students another class session to revise and prepare the final draft for the community viewing.

7 You may opt to create a DVD collection of all the files for the community presentation. Collect the project files in MPEG formats. Click Create Disc and follow the step-by-step tutorial for DVD writing.

Reflections

After learning how to write and produce video narratives, engage students in a discussion of the following.

" What were your highs and lows in the production process? What did you feel good and not feel good about?"

Sample Answers

- Story writing was the most difficult for me. We had to find a way for the elements to come together as one story.

- It's more challenging to have an audience to watch your presentation.

"What did you learn about writing and producing video narratives? What aspect of the lesson made an impact on you? Why? What were the key learning points in the lesson?"

Sample Answer

- I learned about editing and the many ways we can merge creative ideas using the tools of the software.

"What would you have improved if you were given another opportunity to work on the project?"

Sample Answer

- I would have used a better microphone for our shoots.

Summary

- Personal experience is an excellent springboard for writing. The lesson offers students a structure and steps to objectify their life experiences and grow from them. It also keeps them in touch with their experiences.

- Using literary techniques such as metaphors, and analogies and expanding one's vocabulary builds students' skills and expands their imagination to achieve the goal of creating superior literature and multimedia presentations. The application of the elements of art and composition enhances the narrative and articulation of ideas in a multimedia format.

- The non-linear learning strategy frees students from having to write a script first. They can use clay tableaus and the storyboard interface of non-linear editing software like VideoStudio to accelerate the creative writing process.

- By having to prepare for a community viewing, students will be more willing to revise and improve their final products.

- VideoStudio provides an easy-to-use drag and drop editing system. By using this, the teacher need not worry about having students become entangled with the technology or the long and complex procedures of creating an effect or organizing clips. Rather, the GUI provides students the opportunity to focus on the storyline, subject matter, and all the other aesthetic elements that define a great fiction movie.

Building a Classroom Web Site: A Lesson for Teachers

Lesson Objectives

This project will expand instruction and communication beyond the school walls through a classroom web site. Web sites support learning at home through the posting of classroom and homework assignments and facilitate communication and involvement with students and parents.

This chapter outlines simple strategies that enable teachers to create attractive, compelling, and student-oriented web sites. The exercises are designed to guide teachers with no background in web design and who wish to construct their first web pages within the web site of the school.

Skills Learned

Teachers will learn about the four factors involved in designing a classroom web site: vision, content organization, elements of design and composition, and technical applications. The strategies used here build on the creative technology skills introduced in previous chapters, specifically in the use of Photoshop and Word.

Format

The first part of the chapter guides you in defining content and design, after which pages will be brought into web design software called Macromedia Dreamweaver.

Activity 1, Play: Web Site for the Digital Generation

Objectives

- Discover critical facets of the digital generation by finding out their passions
- Scan web resources for information and images that reflect key characteristics of today's digital generation
- Review and expand knowledge of Photoshop and Word. Create a digital image of your typical student by organizing information and images from the web. As design is a strong component of compelling web sites, especially for K–12 students, this activity reviews layers and selection tools.

Instructions

1 Go to a search engine and find three critical concerns and characteristics of today's K–12 generation. Focus on the age group that you teach.
2 Bring these images into Photoshop.

3 Organize images into a digital action figure. Connect the images to the action figure. For example, a cell phone could be halfway in the pocket of a knapsack.

a) Create a new file in Photoshop.

Name:	Digital Action Figure
Width:	5.5 inches
Height:	8.5 inches
Resolution:	150 dpi
Mode:	RGB

b) Find additional images on the Web to form the body of your action figure and bring these into Photoshop.

c) Resize images according to their positions in the action figure. Select the parts of the image with the Polygonal Lasso tool or the Magic Wand. Click Edit, then Transform. By dragging any of the small square shapes around the tool, resize accordingly. You may also use the other tools in the drop-down menu to achieve the most accurate position of the image.

d) Layer your images. Imagine tracing papers one on top of the other. Select the part of the image you wish to manipulate, go to Layer, then New. Name the layer and click OK.

e) Save your file.

Selection Tools

Photoshop provides a variety of selection tools. The Magic Wand is used to select single-colored areas. The Polygonal Lasso tool is used to choose multi-colored and unusually shaped areas. There are selection tools that automatically form a square or rectangle, circle and a line.

Layers and Maneuverability

With the layering tool, Photoshop allows you to create more than 1,000 independent layers in a single file, depending on memory. By layering images, you will be able to manipulate objects more efficiently, without affecting other parts of the picture.

Variation of the Activity

It is always helpful for teachers to find out how students appraise themselves.

1 After working on their digital action figures divide your students into groups of five. They will share their images with groupmates.

As they share, instruct them to make a list of K–12 characteristics brought up by group members.

2 With the large group, discuss the lists written in the small group discussions.

Reflections

You may be working on your own or with a group of teachers. Following are questions that will help crystallize the characteristics of the digital generation, which, in effect, is your target market.

"What is the digital generation so passionate about? Why?"

Sample Answers

- Cellphones, CDs, and MPEG players
- Friends
- Computer games
- Movies

"What differentiates our students from our generation of teachers?"

Sample Answers

- The early exposure to digital media has made them very familiar and comfortable with digital technologies.
- They want immediate gratification.

"What facets of the digital generation should we take into consideration when designing our teacher web sites?"

Sample Answers

- Attractive graphics
- Less text and more pictures for the homepage

Summary

- Almost every student wants to have a CD or MPEG player and to play interactive computer games.
- Our students grew up with computers and the web.
- Most students know how to use computers for word processing, chat, email and interactive games.

- Media dictates fashion trends for the young.

- In designing a web site for K–12 students, we must be aware of what colors, textures, and effects they respond to and create subject matter content in a way that pulls them into the site.

Activity 2, Explore: Design Elements and Organization of Subject Matter

Objectives

- Define your educational philosophy and methodology. Vision determines the form and content of our teaching.

- Create a site map. This is a visual outline of the contents of your curriculum. The titles in the site map must reflect your vision, content, and methods of teaching.

Instructions

1 Search the web for "site map." Click on a web site's site map and review the way they organize their contents.

2 Based on the review and guided by the following questions, create your site map.
   a) Who are your target viewers?
   b) What response do you as a teacher, want from your visitors?
   c) What are the components of your class curriculum?

3 Create your site map using Word or PowerPoint.
   a) Use AutoShape tools to delineate titles in your site map.
   b) Use the Text Box tool to position titles on your project.

4 Save your file. Print a hard copy.

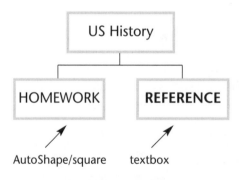

Reflections

Following are questions that will help in the review and enhancement of your site map.

1 What is your vision for learning?
2 How do you intend to deliver this vision in your classroom? What projects will you implement in the first, second, third and fourth quarters?
3 What are your expectations from students?

Summary

- The teacher's vision is reflected in the merging of content, methodology, and classroom delivery.
- The site should reflect learning guideposts in a course.
- The site is the spine of a web site; therefore, it shapes the flow of information.

Activity 3, Integrate: Merge Design with Interactivity

Objectives

The elements of art and composition define the look and usability of a user interface. Use of layers, sizing, and positioning tools are integrated into the elements of art and composition. By playing and experimenting with these elements, one is able to achieve the desired impact.

Instructions

1 Creatively organize the following square shapes in Photoshop.
   - 6 pieces of small-sized squares
   - 3 pieces of medium-sized squares
   a) Go to: www.designworks.com/resources/screen_size_screen_resolution.htm and test the page sizes. Choose the size that best fits your screen.
   b) Go to File, then New. Fill the blanks in the New dialog box according to the page size that best fits your screen. In web

design, a pixel is the unit of measurement used. Standard resolution for web pages is 72 dpi.

c) Create and provide a title of each square piece in a separate layer. Move the pieces around and make sure they form into some kind of aesthetic order.

1 Creatively organize the following circle shapes in Photoshop. Follow the above instructions.

- 5 pieces of medium-sized circles

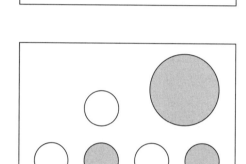

Name:	Square Composition
Width:	800 pixels
Height:	600 pixels
Resolution:	72 dpi
Mode:	RGB

- 1 piece of big-sized squares

2 Save your file. Analyze the look and feel of the visual composition with circles.

Reflections

Following are questions that will help in the review and enhancement of your web site design.

- "What is the first thing that will grab your students' attention in your home page?"
- "How did you apply the elements of visual composition with the circles?"

Summary

- A cursory look into web designs on the Internet will reveal a variety of applications of the elements of art and composition.
- A web site should have a running theme in its use of the elements of art such as shapes, in this case circles.

Activity 4, Imagine: Articulate Your Vision

Objectives

Design your homepage by defining and organizing the visual elements and content highlights of your homepage based on your site map.

Format

There are two sample homepages presented here. The first one is based on circles and will primarily use the image map tool in Macromedia Dreamweaver. The second one is based on squares and rectangles and will primarily use the table tool.

Instructions

A. Design and create web screens in Adobe Photoshop

Sample Web Site 1: Elementary Grades

1   Go to File, then New. Click the small triangle of the drop-down menu bar, choose Custom, and click 640x480 pixels.
    Go to Edit, then Preferences and click Grid. Adjust numbers accordingly:

Gridline:	50 pixels
Subdivisions:	4

Click OK.

2   Create one circle. Go to Layer, then New and name the layer Circle 1. Choose the Elliptical Marquee tool. Go back to your canvas and click and extend the Elliptical Marquee tool to form a 1.25″ diameter circle.

3   Create four more circles. Go to Edit, then Copy. Go to Layer, then New and name the layer Circle 1 and click OK. Do this re-

peatedly until you have five circles, each in separate layers. Name each of your layers accordingly as Circle 2, 3, 4, and 5.

4 Color each of the circles with a transparent look. Pick a color and move the Opacity control bar to 50 percent and then choose the Paint Bucket from the toolbox and click inside the circle. Choose a different color for each of the circles.

5 Create a title for each of your courses. Choose the Type tool. Click on a circle and type the course name. Highlight the course name and customize your font. The parameters of the titles in this homepage are:

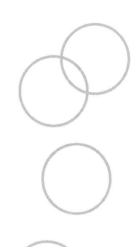

Style:	Bold
Type:	Comic Sans
Size:	24

6 Curve the title. Highlight the title text and choose the Warped Text tool. Click on the arrow to access the drop-down menu at the dialog box. Choose Arc and click OK.

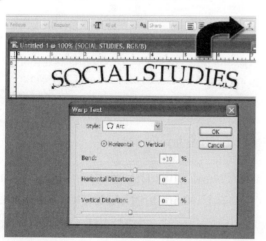

7 Align the curved text within the circle. Click on the text area. For Photoshop Elements, go to Image, then Rotate and click on Free Rotate Layer. Click on one of the square pegs and rotate the text to fit. For Photoshop, go to Edit, then Transform and click Rotate. Click on one of the square pegs and rotate the text to fit.

8 See the illustration below for techniques to insert images and text. Below you have a choice of options for creating images for your site. Save your file after using each of the tools.

Go to Word's AutoShapes tool and choose any shape. Click and extend to create a form. Go to Edit>Copy and bring the shape to Photoshop. Resize to fit the circle. Drag and paste onto the circle.

Go to a search engine and find an image to fit the course title. Copy and paste the image to a new Photoshop file. Use brush and filter tools to alter the image. Flatten the image, drag and paste onto the circle.

Draw on paper, scan the image, and color with Photoshop. Copy and paste.

Photograph a cat and capture the image with Photoshop. Resize and cut out parts to fit the circle. Copy and paste onto the circle.

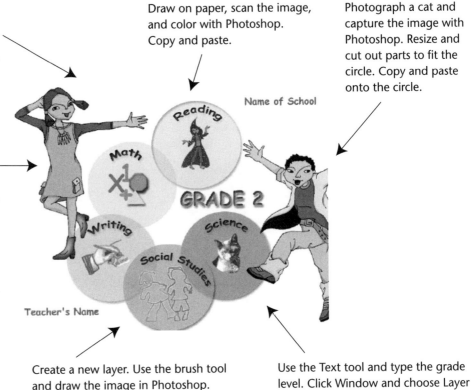

Create a new layer. Use the brush tool and draw the image in Photoshop.

Use the Text tool and type the grade level. Click Window and choose Layer Style. Choose Drop Shadow and Bevel effects.

Sample Web Site 2: High School

1 Go to File, then New. Click the small triangle of the drop-down menu bar, choose Custom and click 800x600 pixels.

2 Go to Edit, then Preferences and click Grid. Adjust numbers accordingly:

Gridline:	50 pixels
Subdivisions:	4

Click OK.

3 Divide the screen into squares. Begin with the big rectangle.

a) Choose the Rectangular Marquee tool and position the cursor on the top left corner of the third square on the grid on the left side of the screen and drag the tool to the right-hand corner, encompassing seven vertical boxes on the grid.

b) Go to Edit, then Stroke. Enter:

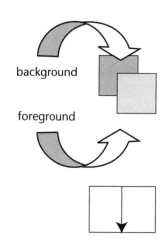

background

foreground

Stroke width:	2 pixels
Color:	Blue
Location:	Center
Blending:	Normal
Opacity:	100%

c) To release the marquee, press Ctrl+D.

4 Divide the big square into small squares.

a) Choose the Rectangular Marquee tool and position your mouse on the top left corner of the fourth square. Drag the cursor to the lower left-hand corner of the fourth box from the right.

b) Go to Edit, then Stroke and click OK.

c) Click the magnifying glass to preview the lines.

d) Choose the Rectangular Marquee tool to form a square from the top-left corner to the middle of the left rectangle.

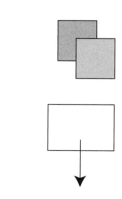

5 Color the squares with the gradient tool.

a) Choose a color for the foreground and another color for the background.

b) Choose the Magic Wand tool and click in the square. Choose the Gradient tool, click and stretch to both vertical ends of the square.

Do the same for squares 1, 2, 3, and 4.

c) For squares 5 and 6, form a square on the top side with the Rectangular Marquee tool. Choose a color for the foreground and another color for the background.

Gradient Tool

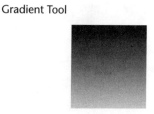

d) Choose the Gradient tool, click and drag to both vertical ends of the square. Do the same with square 6.

6 Add Visual images.

a) Create a new layer. Type a layer name and click OK.

b) Square 1: Grab image from the web, resize, and change color.

c) Square 2: Draw image with the brush tool.

d) Square 3: Grab image from the web, resize and change color.

e) Square 4: Grab image from the web, resize, and use any of your preferred filter tools.

f) Square 5: Grab image from the web, resize, change color, and use filter and brush tools for artistic styling.

7 Add Shadow (Layer Effects)

For Photoshop users:

a) Go to Layer, then Layer Style.

b) Check boxes for desired effects in the Layer Style dialog box and click OK.

For Photoshop Elements users:

a) Go to Window, then Layer Style. The Layer Style dialog box appears.

b) Click the arrow for the drop-down menu.

c) Choose Drop Shadow and Bevel effects and click your preferred effects.

8 Create links for the District and School homepages.

a) Create a new layer and call this District Link or School Link.

b) Choose the Rectangular Marquee tool. Click and drag to form the rectangular button shape. Pick a color and use the bucket to apply inside the square.

c) Apply the Layer Style effects, such as Drop Shadow or Bevel.

Save your File on one folder. All your Web files must be saved on this folder only.

B. Prepare file format for Web integration.

1 Create a duplicate image for each of the screens. Close all original layered images.

2 Accomplish the following for each of the screens. Go to File and choose Save for Web. The Save for Web dialog box appears. Choose one of the images. Preference should be for the image that is lower in resolution so uploading will be faster. However, the aesthetic aspect must also be considered for the site to be visually compelling for the K–12 audience. Click OK and create a New Folder inside the folder you created earlier and title this: Final Web Screens. Give the file a name and click OK.

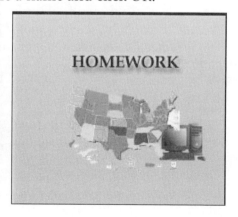

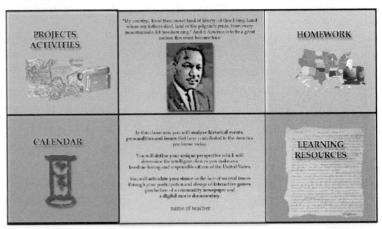

C. Merge screen designs and the outline and content of the course with Macromedia Dreamweaver.

Sample Website 1: Elementary Grades

1 Open Macromedia Dreamweaver MX by clicking its icon. Go to Site and choose New site. The Site Definition dialog box appears. Follow instructions as presented in each dialog box.

2 Write your site name, click Next.

3 Dot the circles: ○ No. I don't want to use a server technology,
click Next. ⟶

   ○ Edit local copies on my machine, then upload to server when ready.

Answer the questions: How do you connect to your remote server? Local/Network

4 Click on the folder where you intend to store ALL your Web site files, click Select and then Next.

5 Dot the option   ◉ No, do not enable check in and check out.
Click Next. ⟶

6   Site summary information will appear. Check information. Click done.

7   Bring the full screen image to Macromedia Dreamweaver MX. Click the Image icon on the task bar. The directory will pop up. Look for the filename of the screen image for example: Grade 2 Class. Open the file and it should open your full screen image in Macromedia Dreamweaver MX.

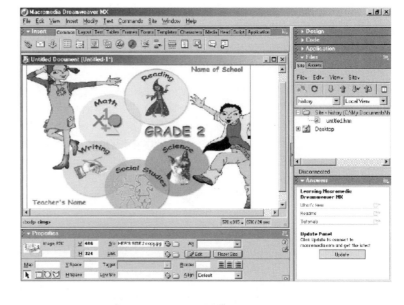

8   Create your inside Web pages. Go to File, choose New and create a Basic HTML Page. Title the page according to the link's name. For example, Social Studies, Math, Reading, and Writing.

9   Create links from the HomePage to the inside pages.

Click on the Polygon Hotspot tool and then bring the cursor to the image link on your screen. Click and stretch and cover the area, defined as your link. On the right-hand side of the link file name box, click on the Point to File tool and connect the line to the Site Directory

hot spot tools

properties bar

specifically to the filename of the page you want to link the image map to. Repeat with the rest of the links and pages.

10 Check the accuracy of your links by clicking the globe icon called Preview/Debug Browser. As soon as the Internet GUI appears with your screen image, mouse over and click to test your links.

11 Save your Site file on the same directory.

Internet Explorer

Netscape

This Web site was designed by Name of Teacher and last updated month/year.

Sample Website 2: High School

1   Follow above instructions from numbers 1-6.

2   Create a Table to structure your Homepage. Click the Table icon on the task bar. The dialog box will appear. Fill the following parameters:

Rows	2	Cell Padding	0
Columns	3	Cell Spacing	0
Width	75 (default) Percent		
Border	0		

and click OK.

3   Insert cut-up images into the Table cells. Go back to Adobe Photoshop/Elements, to the Homepage file.

4   Go to the Toolbox, choose the Rectangular Marquee tool to select acell image. Go to Edit, then Copy to copy and click on the icon of Macromedia Dreamweaver MX on the taskbar. Click the cursor to the corresponding cell and go to Edit, then Paste.

5   Accomplish the same procedure until all six cells are filled with their appropriate images.

6   To link the images and text, follow instructions found in steps 8 and 9 of the previous exercise found in this chapter.

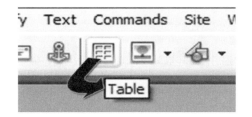

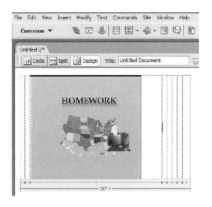

Uploading the Site on the Web

Make arrangements with your school's technology coordinator about hosting your web site. In most circumstances, the teacher supplies the technology coordinator with web pages linked to each other and the coordinator takes care of uploading the pages on the school's web site and linking the teacher's homepage to the school's homepage.

10

Creative Tips and Software Shortcuts

PowerPoint

1 **Create a new PowerPoint presentation using slides created in previous presentations without affecting the first set.** Call the original presentation Slide Set 1 and the new presentation Slide Set 2. Open Slide Set 1 (Ctrl+O on the PC, Cmd+O on the Mac) and create a new presentation (Ctrl+N, Cmd+N). In the Window menu, click Arrange All. You may now copy and paste or drag and drop files between the slide tabs of the two presentations.

PowerPoint

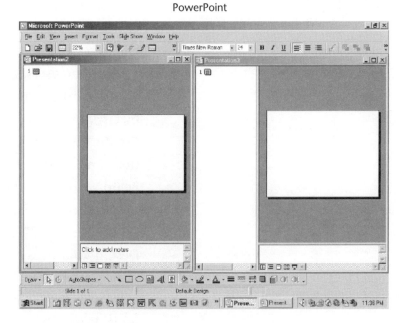

2   **Reorganize your slides from a previous or current presentation.**
Copy and paste slides. Click on the slide you wish to copy on
the slide pane. Go to Edit, then Copy (Ctrl-C, Cmd-C). Click on
the top of the thumbnail slide to position your new slide. Go to
Edit, then Paste (Ctrl-V, Cmd-V).

Delete slides. Click on the slide you wish to delete and press
Delete.

Insert slides. Click on the top of the thumbnail slide to position your new slide. Go to Insert on the toolbar and click New
Slide (Ctrl-M, Cmd M).

3   **Update your Clip Art Gallery with new pictures and media.**
Go to http://office.microsoft.com/clipart/. Click on Click Art
and Media. Click a category. Select a picture by clicking on the
small box below the thumbnail. Click Download Item.

Choose one of the two options for folders to store the item:
2002 or newer or an older PowerPoint version. Click on the version you have on your system. Click Download Now. Choose a
directory.

For PC users, go to drive C, click on Programs, and create a
new folder named WebClipArt. Double-click the folder. Give the
clipart a file name and Save.

For Mac users, go to your Applications folder and follow the
above instructions. Check your art or media file in PowerPoint
by clicking Insert, Picture, Clip Art, then Web Elements.

4   **Create Your Own Background Design Templates for Presentations and Stationeries**
Begin with Adobe Photoshop. Open a new document.

File Size: 11" x 8.5"

Resolution: 72 dpi

Design your background screen to fit the motif or mood of your
presentation. You may choose from colors, textures, and photographs. Experiment with tools such as the gradient and brush
tools. When done, go to Layer on the title bar, and click Flatten
Image. Go to File and Save File As.

There are a few ways to bring your background templates into PowerPoint.

a) Drag and drop

Click Restore on the far right corner on the top blue bar. This tool will provide screen space to view more than one software program. Click and drag into the target PowerPoint slide. Adjust the size of the image with the lower right corner tool marked with diagonal lines. Pulling the image vertically or horizontally may distort your design. If you wish to use this background on a master, drag the image on a slide master. For XP users, you may create several slide masters for your presentation. Go to View on the title bar, click on Master and then Slide Master. You may use any of the following procedures:

- Insert a new slide master
- Delete a slide or title master
- Insert a new title master
- Change the name of a slide or title master

b) Copy and Paste

In Adobe Photoshop: Select the image with any of the marquee tools. Go to Edit, then Copy.

In MS PowerPoint: On the target presentation slide go to Edit, then Paste. Go to Insert, then Picture, then File. Go to the folder and double-click on the file name.

5 **If your screen freezes**

You might have inserted a very large file and your hardware may be slow in processing the commands.

Solution: Wait and be patient. You may consider adjusting image file sizes in Photoshop or if these are photographs, you can also use iPhoto to create smaller file sizes. You may have too many programs open. Programs use memory to run.

Solution (for the PC): Press the Ctrl-Alt-Delete keys all at the same time. Close each of the applications in the pop-up screen. Check to see if PowerPoint works after all software are closed. If not, you need to close PowerPoint and restart your computer. **Solution (for the Mac):** Click and hold each of the software icons on the dock. The option to Quit the software will pop up. Click on Quit on each of the software icons that are opened. Check to see if PowerPoint works after all programs are closed. If not, you need to close PowerPoint and restart your computer. It is my hope that you have saved your file as you made changes on your presentation. The computer will keep the changes you saved.

You may not have enough memory on your hard drive to support the processing of information.
Solution: Memory has gone down in cost. I recommend that you buy more memory. If this is a school computer system, ask the technology support staff to give you a system that has more memory in it.

6 **You want to get rid of the white background in an image you brought in from Photoshop.**

Go to Tools, then Customize. Choose Command. Scroll down and look for Set Transparent Color. Click and drag this command to the toolbar and click OK.

Click on Set Transparent Color and click again on the white area of the image you wish to get rid of. This tool should rid the white background from the image.

7 **You want to get rid of the background design on your master template on one slide of your presentation but do not want to affect all other slides.**

Click on the slide you wish to apply the above changes. Choose Normal View in the bottom left corner of the screen. Go to Format, then Background. In the lower left corner of the dialog box, click on the empty box. A check sign appears. Click Apply or press Enter. If you wish to remove the background design template from all the slides in your presentation, Click the Apply to All button.

8   **You want to control the Timing Effects of your presentation.**

If you intend to use your presentation in class to complement your lecture or any other class activity, you may want to be in more control of the pace by not defining the timing of your slide transitions. In many cases, class situations may require timing adjustment while you are doing the presentation. You will be more in control if you check the On Mouse Click check box.

However if you wish to create a presentation with a life of its own, independent of a lecture or class activity, you may use the timing effects, which usually comes up on display on the right-most column of the XP version of PowerPoint. For the older versions, go to Slide Show and choose Slide Transition. Choose the check box beside Automatically After and then with the vertical-facing arrows, choose the number of seconds you desire for your transitions. If you want timing effects applicable to all transitions in the presentation, click Apply to All. If you want specific transition timing effects for each of the slides, you will have to click on the slide before going to Slide Show. In this way, the Slide Show controls know that you are referring to only that slide.

Dreamweaver

1   **When the link to your district homepage opens you to an error page.**

The link that you typed in the Link box in the properties panel does not match the file name of the page you are trying to link to. It could be either a typo in the file name, you typed in the wrong file name, or the file you are trying to link to is in another folder.

Error page

You have not created the page that the link is meant to take you to. Therefore, the computer cannot find the page. Try this:

Open the homepage in Dreamweaver. Click and drag the mouse pointer across the link that's not working to highlight it.

Go to the Properties Bar at the bottom of your screen. If the properties bar is not there, go to Window, then Properties. The bar will appear. In the Link box in the properties bar, make sure that the file name in the box is the same file name of the page you are linking to. Also, make sure you include the file name extension (.html) in what you typed in the Link box.

Create the web page that you wish to link to. Be sure to save the page under the same file name that you typed into the Link box.

2 **When you can't get your link to work.**

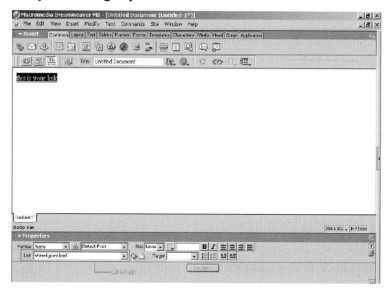
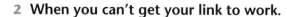

Click and drag the mouse pointer across the link that's not working to highlight it.

Go to the Properties Bar. In the Link box, check the file name for any typos. Check the file name to see if it matches the file name of the page you are linking. Make sure that you include the extension (.html) in the file name.

3 **When the border of the table is too thick and takes up too much in-between spaces.**

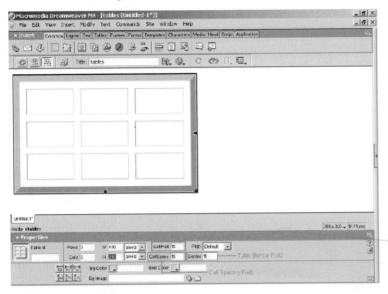

Cause #1:

The Border value in the properties bar is set too high.

Try this: Select the table you wish to modify by clicking once on its border. A bold dark line should surround the table to indicate that it is selected. Next, click inside the border box and change the value of the border's thickness. A higher value means a thicker border, while a lower value results in a thinner border. In order to not have a border, set the border's thickness to 0.

Cause #2:

The cell spacing value in the properties bar is set too high.

Try this: Select the table you wish to modify by clicking once on its border. A bold dark line should surround the table to indicate that it is selected. Click inside the cell space box and change the cell space value. A higher value means a thicker border while a lower value results in a thinner border. To not have cell spacing, set the value to 0. Modifying cell spacing changes the thickness of the interior borders of the table.

Cause #3:

The cell padding value in the properties bar is set too high.

Try this: Modifying the cell padding value does not alter the border's thickness, but rather alters the space between what is inside a cell (text and or pictures) and the border. Select the table you wish to modify by clicking once on its border. A bold dark line should surround the table to indicate that it is selected. In the properties bar, click inside the box labeled cell pad and insert a lower value. A higher value will result in a larger amount of space between what is inside a cell and the table's borders. Setting the value to 0 will create the distance between the contents of a cell and the border to one pixel (the smallest possible distance).

4   **When you can't check your file on the browser.**

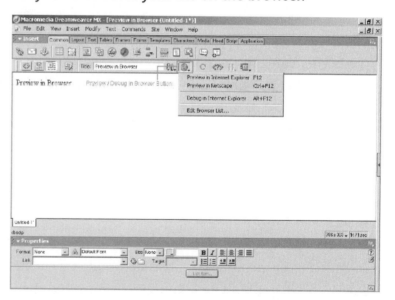

Cause: You have not set a browser for Dreamweaver for file browsing.

Try this: Click the Preview/Debug in Browser button (its icon is the planet Earth) in the Insert toolbar. Click on Edit Browser List. Click the big +.

For Internet Explorer users: Leave the Name field blank for now. In the Application field, click Browse. Look for the Internet Ex-

plorer program in your computer. By default, you start searching inside the Program Files folder. If you are using Windows XP
or ME, Internet Explorer can be found by double-clicking on
the folder labeled Internet Explorer and double-clicking on the
file labeled IEXPLORE.

You will be taken back to the initial window that popped
up. In the Name field, type Internet Explorer. Then click on the
Primary Browser check box (make sure it is checked) and click
OK. You will be taken back to the Preferences window. Click
OK. You will now be able to check your files by clicking on the
Preview/Debug in Browser button on the Insert toolbar. Click
Preview in Internet Explorer.

For Netscape users: Leave the Name field blank for now. In the
Application field, click Browse. You are now going to look for
Netscape Navigator in your computer. By default, you start
searching inside the Program Files folder. If you are using Win-
dows XP or ME, Netscape can be found by double-clicking on
the folder labeled Netscape and double-clicking on a second
Netscape folder that appears, if you have it in your computer.
You will not find a Netscape folder if it is not there.

Double-click on the file labeled Netscape. You are now taken
back to the initial window that popped up. In the Name field,
type Netscape.

Click on the Primary Browser check box (make sure it is
checked), and click OK. You are taken to the Preferences window. Click OK. You are now be able to check your files by clicking on the Preview/Debug in Browser button on the Insert
toolbar and click on Preview in Netscape.

If you cannot see the Insert toolbar, click Window, and see if
the Insert button is unchecked. If so, go ahead and click the
box. If it is not, then the Insert toolbar is somewhere on your
screen, and you may want to move boxes around to find it.

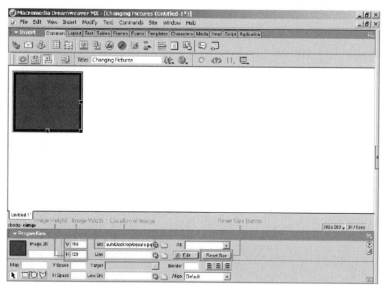

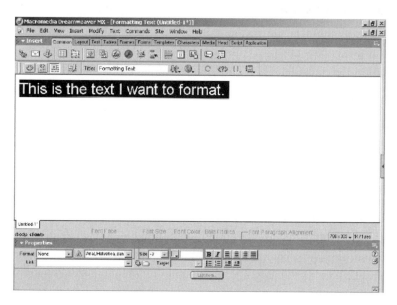

5 **When you want to modify the text and pictures on your pages.**

Select the text. To change the font, leave the text highlighted and click on small arrow inside the Default Font field in the Properties Panel. Select a font from the panel that pops up.

The fonts separated by commas are called font families, and the first font listed in the family is that font you are selecting. The subsequent fonts are substitutions for the first font listed if the first font listed is not installed on the computer of a viewer.

To change the size of text, select the text you wish to modify. In the Properties Panel, click the small arrow inside the Size field and select a size; –7 is the smallest possible size while +7 is the largest possible size. The sizes that are not preceded by a – or + sign are the medium sizes.

To change the color of text, select the text you wish to modify. In the Properties Panel, click the square icon directly to the right of the Size field. A small window will pop up containing a grid of colors. Click once on the square of the color you choose.

To change the paragraph alignment, select the text you wish to modify. On the right side of the Properties Panel, select one of the four paragraph alignment buttons. These are to the right of the Text Color button.

To change text to bold or italics, select the text you wish to modify. In the Properties Panel, click the B or I buttons. If you wish to unitalicize or unbold text, highlight the bold and or italicized text and click the B and or I button again.

To change pictures, select the picture you wish to resize by clicking it once. Once you've done this, a black outline should appear along the edges of the picture. Now, with the picture still selected, look to the Properties Panel.

Just to the right of the field labeled SRC, click the small folder icon. A window will pop up prompting you to find and select the picture you wish to insert. Once you have found the picture, click it once, and then click OK.

To resize a picture, select the picture you wish to resize by clicking it once. Once you've done this, a black outline should appear along the edges of the picture. Now, with the picture still selected, look to the Properties Panel. Located on the left side of the Properties Panel are the W and H fields (W for width, H for height). By changing the values in these fields you will either compress or stretch the picture. Be Careful with Resizing Pictures in Dreamweaver. Enlarging a picture will stretch the image causing pixels to appear, making the picture blurry. Shrinking a picture will not affect picture quality. However, if a picture is shrunk or stretched unproportionally, it will appear to be skewed. To reset a picture to its original dimensions, right-click on the picture once and click on Reset Size in the pop-up menu.

Photoshop

1 **When you can't find the Layers palette.**

For Photoshop, go to Windows, then Show Layers. For Photoshop Elements, go to Windows, then Layers.

2 **When you get the message that your layer is locked.**

Double-click on that layer. This means your layer has been unlocked.

3 **When you want to thicken lines in your image.**

Choose the Zoom tool. Be sure it has the + sign, which means to zoom in. Click on a line area to thicken.

Choose the Magic Wand tool. Bring the pointer on the line area to thicken and click. A selection marquee should appear on the line. To select more lines, hold down the Shift key and bring your pointer to this area and click. Do this again in all the line areas you wish to thicken. Keep the Shift key down until you are done.

When all line areas have been selected go to Edit, then Stroke. A pop-up menu will appear. Choose the thickness by increasing the size of the line. For a thicker line, click the check box beside Outside.

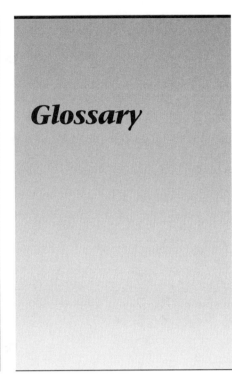

Glossary

Background   The part of the image farthest from the viewer. For image manipulation applications such as Photoshop, the background color refers to the active color for the eraser tool.

Bus   The cables that transmit information. There are internal and external buses that connect to units outside the computer such as digital cameras.

Bytes   One byte is equivalent to eight bits. Memory is measured in bytes.

Camera angle   The position of the camera, which can be from left, from right, from top, from below, or a combination thereof.

Capture   Moving video from a DV camera or a digital camera to a computer. This is achieved with the combined use of a capture device, such as a USB and FireWire cables or capture gadgets and the software interface.

Clips pane   Similar to a library, usually found on the right column of digital video editing software, where footage is organized into clips.

Cross-platform   Software designed for more than one operating system.

Cursor   The movable image onscreen that indicates what the user is working on. Cursor arrow keys on the keyboard or the mouse determine the movement of the image, usually in the form of an arrow.

Cut and paste   To remove a portion of an image and overlay this on another image. This task can also be done from one software application to another.

Deconstruct   To review the parts of something and analyze them.

Desktop system   Hardware and software geared towards printing outputs, including scanner, printer, hardware, and publishing software.

Distill   To separate and extract substance.

Drag   To move an image on the screen. The user will first click on the image and keep the mouse button down and move this to a desired location onscreen.

Dock   On the Mac, as a bar positioned either horizontally or vertically, where software icons are stationed.

DPI   Dots per inch, used to measure image resolution for printers. The higher the dpi, the higher the resolution.

Drop   After an image is moved or dragged from an area onscreen to a desired spot in the graphical user interface, the user lifts the button of the mouse to position that image in place.

Footage   Moving images taken by a video or film camera.

Filter   A transparent material controlling degrees and elements of lighting on an image. In software, there are various types of filters—textures, light, lines, colors, etc.

FireWire   A high-performance cable that can transmit data up to 400 megabits per second. This cable is used for capturing images from a camera to editing software applications.

Foreground   The part of the image nearest to the viewer. For image manipulation applications such as Photoshop, foreground refers to the active color available for the brushes and other painting tools.

Gradient Tool   An image enhancement tool to display the spectrum of colors between two colors. It is found in image software systems like Photoshop.

Hardware   The physical parts of a computer, including mouse, keyboard, CPU, monitor, connectors, etc.

Helix   A spiral image.

Icon   In the graphical user interface, a small image that represents a function.

Image manipulation   Digitally changing features of an illustration, painting or photograph, using graphics software.

Interactive   The ability of a program to accept information from the user, as well as read that data and respond to it in a graphical user interface

Jack (video in and out)   A physical device that connects accessories to the computer and other devices such as DVD and VCR players.

Layer   A vertical overlay on an image, like acetate sheets on top of each other.

LCD (liquid crystal display)   Colors of pixels controlled by light molecules, usually found in watches, projectors, DV cameras, and laptops.

Lens focus   Sharpness or blurriness of the image. It is controlled by the focus ring.

Marketer   One who promotes and advocates a product.

Opacity   Degree of darkness and lightness, or transparency and opaqueness of images.

Pedagogy   A method of teaching.

Pixels   A measurement of images on the monitor; the higher the number the bigger the image.

Play head   An inverted triangle in the scrubber bar of digital video editing software used to view your movies from a beginning to an end point.

Preview screen   An image viewer used to review a movie clip or footage. This is a component of the interface in digital editing software.

Scrollbar   A bar with a sliding rectangle that users manipulate to position an image onscreen to a specific area they are editing.

Search engine   A web site that assists users in locating information in various formats.

Single-platform   Software designed for one operating system, for example, VideoStudio and iMovie.

Software   Programs that instruct the computer to accomplish tasks based on commands determined by a user.

System (as in software and hardware)   Operating mechanisms that control the computer.

Timecode   Appears at the bottom of a video clip and displays the hours:minutes:seconds:frames.

Timeline   A component of video editing software where the system horizontally and vertically arranges clips, transitions, audio, and effects in a movie project.

Tripod   An adjustable stand with three legs for DV cameras to keep the camera steady and for digital cameras to keep the image sharp at lower shutter speeds.

USB   Universal Serial Bus, a protocol that can transmit a 1.5 megabytes per second.

VCR   A video cassette recorder, also called the "play mode" in a DV camera, used to play, fast forward, pause, and rewind footage.

Video clips   Segments of moving images defined by camera on and off boundaries.

Window   A drop-down menu that allows you to access and organize tools on your screen. Window also refers to the organization of images on the screen.

Zoom in   Bringing the image closer and enlarging it onscreen. For movies, it is the camera lens moving from far to near.

Zoom out   Pushing the image further and smaller onscreen. For movies, it is the camera lens moving from near to far.

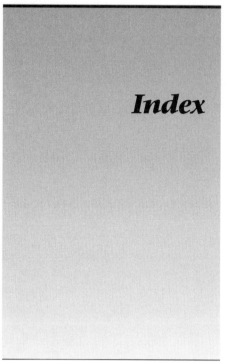

Index

Using the CD

To view the projects on the attached CD-Rom, readers must have Microsoft PowerPoint. To proceed through the slide show, you need to click the down button.

Updates

Want to sign up for e-mail updates for Digital Media in the Classroom? Visit our web site http://www.cmpbooks.com/mail-list and select from the desired categories. You'll automatically be added to our preferred customer list for new product announcements, special offers and related news.

Your e-mail address will not be shared without your permission, so sign up today.

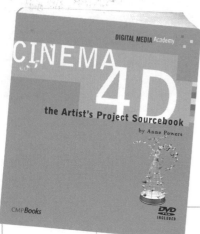

CINEMA 4D
The Artist's Project Sourcebook
Anne Powers

Realize your artistic vision with this treasure chest of instructional projects. This artist's sourcebook is expressly designed for the visionary in you who is looking to make the creative leap with digital tools. You'll learn how to create all kinds of artistic imagery—and have fun in the process. Perfectly suited for classroom use, as well as the self-guided learner, each project is a discrete lesson complete with media supplied on the companion DVD that delivers quick, tangible rewards to keep you learning. Anne Powers is a an award winning fine artist and teacher with a BFA in Fine Art/Painting, an MA in Art Education, and an MFA in Graphic Design with a concentra-tion on Electronic Media. Anne teaches CINEMA 4D in the New Media Academy and Digital Media Academy at Stanford University.

$39.95, Softcover with DVD, 352pp, ISBN 1-57820-242-6

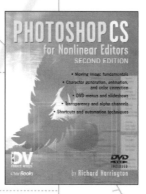

DV Expert Series

Practical, in-depth coverage, for working professionals and aspiring pros. The DV Expert Series delivers the same hands-on techniques and creative approaches that professionals have come to expect from their sister publication, DV magazine. Industry leaders including Trish and Chris Meyer, Jay Rose, John Jackman, Richard Harrington and Tom Wolsky address subjects ranging from lighting and production to editing, motion graphics, audio production, DVD production and compression.

Audience Level: Intermediate to Advanced